M000318011

A Captive Mind

A Captive Mind

Christianity, Ideologies, and Staying Sane in a World Gone Mad

CHRIS NYE

WIPF & STOCK · Eugene, Oregon

A CAPTIVE MIND

Christianity, Ideologies, and Staying Sane in a World Gone Mad

Wipf & Stock
An Imprint of Wipf and Stock Publishers
199 W. 8th Ave., Suite 3
Eugene, OR 97401

www.wipfandstock.com

PAPERBACK ISBN: 978-1-6667-4491-0
HARDCOVER ISBN: 978-1-6667-4492-7
EBOOK ISBN: 978-1-6667-4493-4

All passages of Scripture are from the Holy Bible, English Standard Version (ESV), unless otherwise noted.

This book was professionally typeset on Reedsy. Find out more at reedsy.com

To my mom, who taught me how to think.

People see me all the time
…they just can't remember how to act
Their minds are filled with big ideas
Images and distorted facts

- BOB DYLAN, "IDIOT WIND"

Contents

Preface

I did not plan to write this book. I had a lot of other things I wanted to do. I did some of those things and then I didn't do other things I probably should have done. But this book has possessed me. I was taken over by its urgency and importance and, well, here it is.

I also didn't plan to write this book because it didn't start as a book. I wrote a series of articles that didn't really have a home anywhere else on the internet or in print. In looking back on some of those pieces, I realized much of it was around the same theme: *why and how should I remain a wise Christian when everyone seems crazy? How do I make sense of my faith inside a world that makes no sense at all?*

This book is a collection of writing I've done around ideology. How and why have so many people adopted sets of ideas from conservative and liberal circles, not realizing they are, at the same time, abandoning biblical Christianity? Between the influence of new, pseudo-intellectuals on social media and the rise of partisan media corporations, it seems as if we have more invitations to adopt beliefs quickly instead of forming them over time. In what ways can we be faithful Christians when the world is going crazy? Or—wait a second—before we answer all of those, maybe we should ask: are *we* crazy? Have we unknowingly fallen captive to some ideological prison?

You may have picked up this book because you saw the

subtitle or description and you got all pumped up: you think everyone else is insane and you're in the clear. You look out at "the world" or "the culture" and think…man, *people* are crazy. As I will argue in this book, I think that is a spiritually dangerous place to be. The first step towards complete ideological captivity and dull-headed Christianity is to believe it could never be true of you. Vigilance over our minds and souls—avoiding what is often called "stubbornness of heart"—is a spiritual discipline deep in the people of God (Deuteronomy 29:18-19, Jeremiah 7:24). I will repeat this several times in the book because I'm afraid that is largely unspoken in Christian circles: you can become foolish faster than you think. The certainty with which believers approach information, the arrogance that can come inside certain insidious theological and philosophical streams, is so widespread right now that I am making the tiniest effort to push against it. We need humility, careful thinking, and prayerful understanding of our small place in a very big and complicated world. The craziness is not "out there."

What you have before you is an edited and expanded version of the haphazard writing that's been done over the past few years. If you follow my work closely, you will read familiar things in here, but you will also read brand new stuff too. Seven of these twelve chapters have never seen the light of day, and the remaining ones were only self-published on the internet in their infant form. This is all to say that this book is quite new. The ideas in here needed time to mature and take a better shape. I hope I've given them enough time, but I'm also sure I haven't.

I have two dominating passions in this project that I might as well tell you about right now in a plain manner. First, I have an overwhelming desire to convince the Church to remain: to remain Christian, to remain wise, to remain together. Perseverance, wisdom, and unity are not only scarce today, but they are not handled with care. The snark of the internet and the cynicism inside the zeitgeist has carried us as a culture into a place of leaving things easily, especially leaving Christianity. I would love to be involved in a humble effort towards a united and faithful Church.

There are a cacophony of resources, blogs, books, and podcast episodes about leaving Christianity, questioning religion, and moving right into the culture's nucleus. I do not think there are enough pastors and writers providing compelling reasons to remain a thoughtful, humble Christian presence in the world.

Secondly, I want to encourage and help Christians who look around with despair. I consider despair to be one of the more debilitating spiritual conditions we can experience. It is paralyzing. I hope this book helps Christians make sense of a crazy world. This is not the first time the world has gone mad, and it will not be the last.

Aside from these two reasons, there are also two passages of Scripture you will find repeated throughout this book: Colossians 2 and 1 Corinthians 1-2. For the richest experience in reading this book (and in life in general), please read and pray through those chapters as you make your way through this little volume. I'm serious. Go. Do it.

Ok. Having stated these things plainly, I also have long been at peace with the fact that many disciples wander off (John 6:66). Not all seeds produce lasting fruit (Matthew 13:1-8). This has been a simple fact of the Jesus Way since before Jesus walked the earth. Getting out from under the ways and wisdom of the living God is the very fabric of sin itself. Adam and Eve left God's wisdom in light of a lie presented to them about reality.

xi

Jesus' own followers left him. The church has had millions of apostates. So let's not expect a short book like this to solve a problem so deeply intertwined with the human race.

I'd like to, instead, look at a compelling vision for life. Christianity is rarely what we think it is. Following Jesus does not involve constant intellectual and emotional affirmation. Rather, he comes to us as a surprise. We do not follow him because it always makes sense, or because it fits perfectly with our cultural lenses—discipleship rarely, if ever, does this. Instead we follow Jesus because, like Peter, we see no other option. Where are the teachings that lead to a full life? Where is salvation? We are not in need of "good ideas" or "something helpful," as we would find in an article or podcast—no—we are on the hunt for something far more dangerous and transcendent, something that comes from another dimension, another plane of existence. Where, my friends, is eternal life? May we find it only in Jesus Christ.

> [60] When many of his disciples heard it, they said, "This is a hard saying; who can listen to it?" [61] But Jesus, knowing in himself that his disciples were grumbling about this, said to them, "Do you take offense at this? [62] Then what if you were to see the Son of Man ascending to where he was before? [63] It is the Spirit who gives life; the flesh is no help at all. The words that I have spoken to you are spirit and life. [64] But there are some of you who do not believe." (For Jesus knew from the beginning who those were who did not believe, and who it was who would betray him.) [65] And he said, "This is why I told you that no one can

come to me unless it is granted him by the Father."

⁶⁶ After this many of his disciples turned back and no longer walked with him. ⁶⁷ So Jesus said to the twelve, "Do you want to go away as well?" ⁶⁸ Simon Peter answered him, "Lord, to whom shall we go? You have the words of eternal life, ⁶⁹ and we have believed, and have come to know, that you are the Holy One of God."

-John 6:60-69

Finally, a brief note about the title. Some readers may note that the title of this book (*A Captive Mind*) sounds familiar beyond its colloquial significance. This is because it resembles (and is quite near) the title of Czesław Miłosz's *The Captive Mind* (with the noted, more precise definite article), first published in English in 1953. Miłosz was a Polish Soviet defector, whose poetry and prose won him the Nobel Prize. His monograph, which is probably far more prophetic and well-written than this one, was not an influence in this simply because I have not read it. I only heard about it when I Googled this title of which I was fond. However, being that Miłosz's book is all about the allure Stalinism had on his country (particularly the upper-classes), and the ways in which ideologies inform totalitarianism, I suppose I was right on the nose. I acknowledge the now deceased Miłosz here, only to say sometimes coincidences do not detract from meaning, but enhance it.

1

When the content consumes you

"They say I got brains
  But they ain't doing me no good
  I wish they could"
    -The Beach Boys, "I Just Wasn't Made for These
                                              Times"

* * *

I'm on my back deck, eating a cheeseburger out of a to-go container, as Preston (not his real name) tells me about his friend who has "gone full MAGA." We're talking about what you do when the person you've known for years suddenly becomes a parrot for a political ideology (you've been here too, right?). Preston talks about how you've got to choose your friends and, while he used to be able to talk to this guy about any number of things, he cannot separate his friend's political beliefs from everything else about their relationship. When

1

your friend has become a walking retweet of internet garbage, it's hard to even talk to them about the weather.

"Was he always like this?" I asked, knowing the answer.

"No...only since he took his new job."

Of course he wasn't always like this. Of course he didn't say the things that he says now. This is because no one else was saying these things he was saying until quite recently. This is also because Preston's friend is a parrot. A parrot repeats catchphrases, regurgitates hot takes, and, of course, retweets predictable voices. A parrot does not think.[1] And so how could he? If the way you communicate your opinion sounds exactly like any number of media figures, podcasters, or social media influencers, it turns out you don't have opinions at all; you've got a script. This is an ideological prison, when one's mind is held captive by a set of ideas prescribed to a public ready to receive them. This person has stopped consuming content and has let the content consume them.

Once someone has been consumed by media content, they have entered ideological captivity: they are no longer a thoughtful person, able to parse information and make rational sense of their beliefs or humbly engage in contradicting opinions with genuine interest. They do not slowly think through how they might be wrong or what they might be missing. Instead, they search for "information" that is not information at all, but rather bits of data that matches their temperament of fear, anger, and suspicion. And you've seen it: very few people have *thoughts* anymore, but they have *feelings about thoughts*. Rational ideas

---

[1] I'm realizing I don't know a lot about parrots. They're probably super smart, but when this word is applied to humans, it means they're not. Can we just roll with it and not get into the specifics behind ornithological brain science? Thanks.

and critical thinking has been replaced with catchphrases that identify our emotions on our behalf, which leads us to repeat those catchphrases and pass them along:

"The government is taking our freedom!"
"This is the seeds of totalitarianism..."
"This is fascism!"
"This is socialism!"
"Before we know it, we'll be in Stalinist Russia..."
"Before we know it, we'll be under a fascist dictator..."

And those are just political examples from this year.[2] The thing about these catchphrases is that they are not opinions or even coherent thoughts. They are a representation of a person's emotional experience about the world. In modern America, we have now disguised our feelings with language that *sounds like* we're thinking. But we're not thinking at all. We're just feeling a lot of things.

* * *

My friend Preston tells a common story with a question at the center of it: how do you stay wise when the world has gone crazy? As a pastor, I engage in all kinds of conversations, trying to help people understand God's relationship with the world. I cannot tell you how many conversations I have had like this

---

[2] Even though I have heard Christians say these things, I have refrained from citing specifically "Christian" examples because I'd rather get political people mad than Christian people. You too, right? Also, it's been interesting for me to hear both those on the right *and* the left accuse each other of "fascism" and "Stalinism," which makes me think both sides understand neither.

over the past 6-7 years. Everyone thinks everyone *else* is crazy. And we're all trying to figure out if maybe there's a way we can stay wise.

And this is what concerns me. If everyone thinks everyone else is crazy, how can we be certain we've avoided the insanity ourselves? The first step towards what I will call "ideological captivity" (what we generally call "going crazy") is to believe that you could never experience it yourself. To think you'll never be a fool is to admit you already are one. And it is precisely this arrogance that I sensed in myself that got me to start writing about it all. How can we stay wise, humble, and thoughtful when so many are foolish, proud, and quick? How can we consume content without the content consuming us? People have always been foolish, but it seems we're under a fresh storm of idiocy in the "developed" world. The internet has perhaps opened us up to all kinds of crazy at one time, as we watch people deny a reality they are emotionally unprepared to meet.

"Ideological captivity" is the slow but certain hardening of our mind and heart when approaching new information. It happens when we only consider one kind of source, or one algorithm of content on YouTube or Twitter. We consume enough Instagram posts, podcasts, and articles from the same stream of thinking that we end up only thinking within that stream only. And then we're trapped. To have our minds held captive by one *way* of thinking about the world is to be inside an ideological prison.

* * *

Teeming inside of many Americans is the notion that their feelings are the most important thing about them—the era of the "psychological man," as Philip Rieff has deemed it, is upon us.[3] To the modern Western person, Rieff argues, the world exists as a place to reflect how I feel...and how I feel about how I feel. As David Wells has argued, in this world:

> "Theology becomes therapy....The biblical interest in righteousness is replaced by a search for happiness, holiness by wholeness, truth by feeling, ethics by feeling good about one's self. The world shrinks to the range of personal circumstances; the community of faith shrinks to a circle of personal friends. The past recedes. The Church recedes. The world recedes. All that remains is the self."[4]

The modern person exists to be emotionally understood. If they are not, they cease to be able to articulate meaning and, to them, they might as well be dead. *If I cannot tell you how I feel, I am nothing.* Our god is our heart.[5] We seek out a political or cultural ideology through ideas that make us feel a type of

---

[3] Philip Reiff, *The Triumph of the Therapeutic: Uses of Faith after Freud* (Intercollegiate Studies Institute, 2006).

[4] David Wells, *No Place for Truth: or Whatever Happened to Evangelical Theology?* (William B. Eerdmans Publishing, 1994), p. 183

[5] A decent historical summary of this is provided by Carl R. Trueman in *The Rise and Triumph of the Modern Self: Cultural Amnesia, Expressive Individualism, and the Road to Sexual Revolution* (Crossway, 2020). It is unfortunate that Trueman's conclusions (especially around sexuality and gender) are misplaced and include too many logical leaps by which I could never be convinced. While he and I agree on the historic, orthodox view of sexuality and gender, the routes he gets there are concerning and overly simplified to me.

way: secure, understood, safe, happy, etc. We do not think thoughts and tell other people what we think because we've arrived rationally and humbly at that place, but because we have arrived there emotionally. To be empathized with ("I need to feel seen" or "he/she just gets me") is the goal of modern life.[6]

This is the beginning of what I will call "ideological captivity."[7] Ideologies are sets of ideas, often put together by an amalgamation of cultural events, leading charismatic thinkers, and now, algorithms. These ideas are organized and then presented and re-presented until they are ingratiated into the zeitgeist. The word "ideology" is credited to Antoine Destutt de Tracy, who wrote in French after the revolution. He "intended to create a proper brand of study concerned with ideas… to establish ideals of thought and action on an empirically verifiable basis."[8] But it was really Karl Marx and Friedrich Engels who would take the meaning of the word into its modern, political context. For Marx and Engels, the "German Ideology" was the effort to exchange illusory thought for correct thought, thereby creating catch phrases that represented larger ideas, without the complexity, length, and nuance.[9]

At the moment of their insistence to the larger culture—when the YouTube videos, podcasts, publishing houses, and social media platforms are aflame with their pandering—viewers give

---

[6] This is (more or less) what Alasdair MacIntyre calls "emotivism," for more see MacIntyre, *After Virtue: A Study in Moral Theory*, Third Edition (University of Notre Dame Press, 2007), pgs. 23-35.

[7] I certainly did not invent this term, but no one really knows who did or didn't. So I'm just using it; I'm not claiming to have coined it.

[8] Michael Freeden, *Ideology: A Very Short Introduction* (Oxford University Press, 2003), pg. 4

[9] Freeden, *Ideology*, pgs. 1-5.

ideologies little-to-no criticisms. Then, they adopt these sets of ideas wholesale. No thinking necessary; the ideas are set. As Aziz Ansari has said, if someone shares *one* opinion with him, he already knows the rest of what they think about most everything else. They're stuck in an algorithm, not a mind.[10] In a world of ideologies, when you buy one idea, chances are the rest of that particular set gets thrown in for free. If you're not careful or humble, you buy one and get them all.

Many in ideological captivity adopt a set of catch phrases and prepackaged opinions not out of reason, but emotion. When emotional expression is paramount, why critique an idea if it matches my emotions? The only reason your uncle became obsessed with conspiracy theories or your cousin became a socialist or your friend went all-in on populism was because someone (or many someones) in the landscape of their media experience probably made them *feel* a certain way. Ideology famously clothes our emotions in simplistic logic: "this is the way life is" or "don't you miss the days when_____?" or "_____ is stopping human progress." After that, the key is thrown out and we're locked away. Our mind is no longer free after we sold it to someone else. Except with this kind of captivity, the lock is not on the outside of the cell, but the inside. Any time we'd like, we can go free. But we won't. It feels too good to be "right."

And that is what is making me think about Preston's friend and about that cheeseburger I was eating on my back deck. In today's world, there are so many brains but there are no

---

[10] Aziz Ansari, *Nightclub Comedian* (2022), Netflix.

minds.[11] Wisdom, decision-making, careful thought, and intentional reflection through prayer and worship are all very, very rare right now, but are all nevertheless necessary for a free mind.

* * *

The writers of Scripture assumed their readers could fall prey to all sorts of mental traps. We're all susceptible to ideological captivity. As we'll discuss in the next chapter, "foolishness" is not just a theme in the Old Testament Wisdom Literature, rather the Wisdom Literature serves as a window in to the whole Bible's emphasis on becoming and staying wise because *all people* are tempted to become fools.[12] The Bible is full of sharp warnings about drifting from the True God into strange myths (1 Timothy 1:4), astrological obsessions (Deuteronomy 4:19, Job 31:26-28), bad philosophies (Colossians 2:8), deceitful and meaningless words (Ephesians 5:6), useless conversations (1 Timothy 4:7, 6:20), and also says a lot about keeping our distance from bad teachers (Deuteronomy 18:15-22, Jeremiah 5:31, 27:15, Ezekiel 13:1-9, Matthew 7:15, 24:24, Luke 6:26, 1 Timothy 1:3, 2 Peter 2:1, 1 John 4:1).

But verses like these are often quoted and used in a superficial way. We're told to simply *think* different things: stop thinking

---

[11] For more, see Marilynne Robinson, *Absence of Mind: The Dispelling of Inwardness from the Modern Myth of the Self* (The Terry Lectures Series), (Yale University Press, 2011).

[12] For more of an academic treatment on the limitations of categorizing the Wisdom Literature and the problems that have arisen because of it, see Will Kynes, *An Obituary for "Wisdom Literature": The Birth, Death, and Intertextual Reintegration of a Biblical Corpus* (Oxford University Press, 2019).

about worldly stuff and think about eternal things; avoid false things by thinking true things; combat bad lies with good truth nuggets from God's Word. I want to be generous to this kind of teaching. There is room for eliminating lies with Bible verses; I believe that is a valuable practice, to some extent. There are moments in discipleship to Jesus where one lie needs to be combated with one piece of truth that contradicts it. But some of the strongest verses about wise thinking are actually not teaching this kind of thing at all. They're saying something much more evocative and interesting.

Christianity, as we'll see fully in chapter 3, is not a set of right ideas that combat and defeat bad ideas. Our faith is not a set of truths (plural), but The Truth (singular) revealed in Jesus Christ. "The Christian story," according to C.S. Lewis, "is about a historical personage, whose execution can be dated pretty accurately...It is not the difference between falsehood and truth. It is the difference between a real event on the one hand and dim dreams or premonitions of that same event on the other."[13] Christianity is not a philosophy,[14] but a thunderous arrival of the Living God in Jesus Christ upon the heart, mind, and soul of the human being who responds to him. The Christian message is, as Lesslie Newbigin writes, "the announcement that in the series of events that have their center in the life, ministry, death, and resurrection of Jesus Christ something has happened that alters the total human situation and must therefore call

---

[13] C.S. Lewis, "Is Theology Poetry?" in *The Weight of Glory* (HarperCollins, 2001), pgs. 128-129.

[14] Although there is "Christian philosophy," the entirety of Christianity is not philosophical. Our Christianity *informs* our philosophical ideas—it shapes them and rearranges them—but its nature is not philosophical. See chapters 3-4 for more.

in to question every human culture."[15] This would include ideologies. This personal and cosmic arrival of Jesus does not come through correct thinking, but through a move of the Holy Spirit that rattles our human experience and thereby changes how we think about everything.[16]

Christianity is not some new set of glasses that slightly corrects our blurry vision of life. Christianity is the ability to see after having been completely blind. Our very posture and attitude towards the world is never the same after being arrested by the love of God. We do not just "see things differently" now; we see for the very first time. We were blind and now we see (John 9:25, 2 Corinthians 4:3-6). We are not converted by an idea or sets of ideas that slightly corrects our worldview; we actually view the world for the first time after having met Christ. We are converted by the person of Jesus through the power of the Holy Spirit. God *happens to us* and we convert. We do not, then, fight lies with truths (in a one-for-one exchange of bad lies for good truths); we fight lies with The Truth of who Jesus Christ is, what he has done, and who he is to us today as he lives and reigns.

Perhaps a picture can help us: C.S. Lewis famously spoke of

---

[15] Lesslie Newbigin, *Foolishness to the Greeks: The Gospel and Western Culture* (Wm. B. Eerdmans Publishing Co., 1986), pgs. 3-4.

[16] When people are converted in the New Testament (and today, for that matter), it is clear that something is *happening* to them. Christians can often tell you how they became Christians and certainly where and when, but very few can tell you *why*. The beautiful unique feature of Christian conversion is that every conversion is God's idea and God's initiative. For more see Richard V. Peace, *Conversion in the New Testament: Paul and the Twelve* (Wm. B. Eerdmans-Lightning Source, 1999). For a more pastoral and personal academic reflection, see Gordon T. Smith, *Beginning Well: Christian Conversion & Authentic Transformation* (IVP Books, 2001).

believing Christianity as one believes in the sun rising: "not only because I see it, but because by it I see everything else."[17] Consider the resurrection of Jesus Christ as the rising of the sun. Before it, everything is dark and nothing can be seen. But as we look upon this event—and we look upon it because we cannot help but look—we also see its permeating power to see all other things. Without that event, there is no sight. But with this event, with the God Who Rose, we can see so much with clarity and humility. Our friends will argue about ideas on all sides and we will engage with those ideas—we'll read the article they sent and take in the podcast—but we'll do it with a perspective that comes from our faith, not mistaking our faith for the idea they are presenting.

The more we walk with Jesus, it will become silly to argue about the importance of ideas in the same way that it would be idiotic to argue about a rock when considering the massive importance of the sun. We would never see the rock had it not been for the sun. It is good to look upon, it is interesting to consider, but our very life is not dependent on it the way it is upon the sun.

Another helpful metaphor is much more biblical: the kingdom. While we will explore the kingdom more in depth in chapter 9, employing it here is helpful. The "kingdom of God" is not so much a metaphor as it is a reality, but the term "kingdom" helps us see what Jesus' main message was all about. The main message of Christ was "Repent, for the kingdom of God is at hand" (Matthew 3:2, 4:17, 10:7, Mark 1:15). The kingdom is the place where God's will is being done,

---

[17] C.S. Lewis, "Is Theology Poetry?" in *The Weight of Glory* (HarperCollines, 2001), pg. 140.

where his power is the primary animating feature of a particular space. The kingdom "breaks in" to this world and comes from another (which is why Jesus often refers to it as "the kingdom of heaven"). As Christians, we exist in that space and no longer exist in the kingdoms "of this world" or "of darkness." We've been transferred (Colossians 1:13-14). The entire operating principles of this kingdom are different than the kingdoms of this world (see Matthew 5:1-16). It's "upside down" from our world.[18]

Christians are "citizens" of God's kingdom (Ephesians 2:19, Philippians 3:20). To be a citizen is to be cultured by a certain place and people group. Who you are—your norms, habits, ideas about life—comes from where you live. If you grow up in China as a Chinese citizen, you will not act like a citizen from Mexico. You both come from different cultures so you are vastly different people with unique ways of living and thinking. Christians live their life inside the alternate reality—another place—called "the kingdom of God," thereby holding a whole different set of beliefs and ideas that will seem foreign to those who live in earthly kingdoms and cultures. It would be strange if citizens of the kingdom of God had the exact same cultural expressions as any worldly kingdom simply because of the originating place of both kingdoms. "My kingdom is not of the this world," Jesus says (John 18:36), and therefore the citizens of this kingdom will act and think in ways that do not fit with the citizens of other kingdoms. Citizenship in the kingdom will not match the ideologies developed by citizens of this world.

---

[18] Nearly everything I say about the kingdom of God is a direct result of reading Dallas Willard.

* * *

The clearest depiction of this is in the book of Colossians: "See to it," Paul warns the church, "that no one takes you captive by philosophy and empty deceit, according to human tradition, according to the elemental spirits of the world, and not according to Christ" (Colossians 2:8). Notice that the test for avoiding ideological captivity ("captive by philosophy") is to inspect what you are hearing and see if it is "according to Christ."[19] Do these various ideas and thoughts live harmoniously with who I know Jesus to be from Scripture? How is what I am listening to in accord or discord with Jesus Christ as revealed in Scripture? To employ the aforementioned metaphor, in what ways does the light of the sun (Jesus) hit this rock (whatever idea we're listening to)? This means when we encounter ideas, we do not fact check them with Scripture or grab one verse that would "support" or "dismiss" the idea; we actually take the entirety of the Biblical narrative as seen through Christ and interact with that idea based on our relationship with him. This will mean we are both more open and generous to new ideas and more fiercely committed to the convictions of Christianity.[20]

Paul says we will hear all kinds of lies—some human ("according to human tradition") and some demonic ("according to the elemental spirits of this world"). His answer for a world of

---

[19] "The unusual [Greek] word used [for "take captive"] here speaks of the slave-raider carrying off his victim, body and soul. These plausible teachers may say that they come to bring Christians new liberties but, says Paul in effect, don't go near them if you value your spiritual freedom." Dick Lucas, *Fullness & Freedom: The Message of Colossians & Philemon* (InterVarsity Press, 1980). The Bible Speaks Today. Accessed on Logos Bible Software.

[20] Trust me, the rest of this book will show you how to do this.

crazy ideas is not a bunch of good Christian ideas (something like, "the world is telling you to divorce your spouse, quote the Bible's teaching to stay married!"). His entirely different answer is found in the very next verse: "For in Christ the whole fullness of deity dwells bodily, and you have been *filled in him, who is the head* of all rule and authority" (Colossians 2:9, emphasis mine).[21] He then goes on to explain the power and meaning of what happened on the cross (Colossians 2:10-15) and imploring his church to set their minds on the truth that is "*above*, where Christ is, seated at the right hand of God" (Colossians 3:1, emphasis mine).

Notice the location and the person in that last verse. Paul admonishes the church to look both somewhere else and at someone else. Our faith does not exist in this dimension nor does it rest on ideas from this world. We are to pull our whole attention beyond what we can see towards the One who has given us sight in the first place. The bodily raised and ascended Jesus Christ does not sit in competition with ideas about life and politics, he sits above them in power. To be a Christian in a world of ideologies is not to primarily "go to war" with bad ideas, but to worship the One True God who sits above them, destroying them with his singular, revealed truth. Christians know truth because they know the Truth, who is the person

---

[21] The Church Father John Chrysostom acknowledges the surprise of Paul's move here: "such a solution [to combating bad philosophy] is not suspected." See John Chrysostom, "Homilies of St. John Chrysostom, Archbishop of Constantinople, on the Epistle of St. Paul the Apostle to the Colossians." *Saint Chrysostom: Homilies on Galatians, Ephesians, Philippians, Colossians, Thessalonians, Timothy, Titus, and Philemon.* Ed. Philip Schaff. Trans. J. Ashworth and John Albert Broadus. Vol. 13. New York: Christian Literature Company, 1889, pg. 285. A Select Library of the Nicene and Post-Nicene Fathers of the Christian Church, First Series.

called Jesus, the Son of God.

To think rightly in this world, we do not need more good ideas, we need a vision from another world, a revelation. We need to see Jesus Christ—how his life, death, resurrection, and ascension changes the fundamental vision of human reality, thereby leading us into all truth. Christianity is a faith from another dimension; ideologies and philosophies sit beneath its power. It's really just a matter of ordering our steps as Christians: acknowledging the living reality of Jesus comes before we parse out what is true and what is not because he, himself, and all that is in him, remains the standard of all truth for all time. Simply put, what we need before proper thinking is proper worship.[22]

This is why Paul's letter to the Colossians is so helpful. The first three-and-a-half chapters are his musings on the truth of who Jesus is and what he has done. He invites his readers to worship and adore Christ as risen and reigning. The final chapters, then, are instructions on how to live rightly *in light of* who Jesus currently is (Colossians 3:5-4:18). As I will argue throughout this book, Christianity does not have an ideology or worldview as a starting point (or really ever, for that matter). We Christians have Jesus Christ risen from the dead. This—and only this—is the fount from which every other true thing we

---

[22] Lucas comments on the proper ordering of worship and then thinking: "Of course Paul is not content simply to label the new teaching as harmful and misleading; the whole situation gives him an opportunity, not to be missed, to expound the treasures that already belong to those in Christ. Once the Colossians understand their position of privilege in Christ, it is inconceivable that they will want to look elsewhere than to Christ for spiritual satisfaction." Dick Lucas, *Fullness & Freedom*. Accessed on Logos Bible Software.

have to say comes. We would not say what we say about marriage, justice, finances, relationships, etc. had Jesus not lived, died, and raised on the third day. Everything hinges on him and everything comes from him.

* * *

What we often think next is, "Well, isn't Christianity just a set of ideas, too? Aren't Christians just following a 'Christian' ideology?" Isn't Christian doctrine just an ideology itself?

There is a fundamental difference in terms that we should address right away, and that is the difference between doctrine and ideology. The "ideas" about Christianity are not, in the end, mere ideas. They have long been claimed by the Church as *doctrine*, which is a way of thinking with far different roots than ideologies. They are not just different words for the same thing, they are different entities in their nature.

Ideologies—by their very definition—are organized and arranged by human beings. They are the creations of the created, and therefore the Creator stands above them.[23] Ideologies are not doctrines. Doctrines are truth statements based off of scriptural texts that report divine events and instructions from the Living God. Ideologies are the organized ideas of human beings through socio-philosophical inquiry. Doctrines are

---

[23] I am well aware that this argument is founded upon Theism. If you're wrestling with the existence of God or unsure, the theological framework of most of the arguments in this book might be frustrating, but I would encourage you (in the spirit of rejecting ideological captivity) to continue reading and even pray. If you're looking for a great and modern case for Christian Theism, please see Gavin Ortlund, *Why God Makes Sense in a World That Doesn't: The Beauty of Christian Theism* (Baker Academic, 2021).

revealed; ideologies are invented. Doctrines come as a surprise while ideologies make perfect sense in the culture in which they were formed. Doctrines are unearthed from Spirit-scripted texts; ideologies are constructed from man-made ideals. They are fundamentally different in origin: doctrine comes from God by our listening and ideologies come from human beings 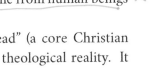 by our invention.

To say "Christ is risen from the dead" (a core Christian doctrine) is to affirm a historical and theological reality. It is a belief connected to an event. This claim lies in the world of metaphysics, if it lies in any world at all. We are claiming something physical that transcends physicality; we are talking about a historical event that pulls back the curtain on all of history. It is emphatically *not* an idea. This is a doctrine that has arrived to us through events and people that claimed those events had a theological meaning only God could show us. After having listened, the doctrines arrived.

* * *

So what? Why does all of this matter and how can it lead us to not join in on the craziness?

Think about this with me: if all of our thinking begins with worship and the acknowledgment of God's reality in Jesus Christ, then there's so much space for freedom, disagreement, and mind-changing in the church. If Christianity is not a set of ideas, then the sets of ideas we do form can be more generous than we may initially think. If we hold fast to our doctrine, the ideas that come from the world can easily come in and out of our lives with relatively low stakes—at least lower than many alarm-ringers today claim.

If we properly understand that *doctrine* is to be guarded, then *ideas* become interesting subjects with real world consequences for sure, but they do not become the life and death of the Church. We can talk about immigration and abortion policy, or Just War Theory, or the climate crisis, or college campus bathrooms with a kind of humility and generosity because we do not see these ideas or policies as something that can upend our Christianity. If our faith is based on a historical reality articulated through doctrines, then Christianity can never be threatened. Events are not called into question by ideas. Either something happened or it did not. Certainly the *meaning* of that event can and will be discussed and interpreted, but its very nature is not under threat. Ideas are playing a different game than doctrines.

Of course, there are doctrines in Christian faith that make Christianity "Christian." Our faith affirms that certain things are true. But every one of these truth convictions are based inside the event of the resurrection. As Paul famously and provocatively says, "[I]f Christ has not been raised, then our preaching is in vain and your faith is in vain" (1 Corinthians 15:14). When I say that Christianity is not an idea, but an event (the life, death, and resurrection of Jesus), this certainly means that we must affirm some doctrines about that specific event. But again, these are *doctrines* and not ideas. An idea can exist apart from the resurrection and a doctrine cannot. Many Christians get angry, upset, and even volatile over ideas that are not in any way connected to Christian doctrine or the resurrection. This is one way some have stepped into ideological captivity.

The doctrines cleanly and closely connected to the resurrection are what we call "essential" or "primary" doctrines. Essential and primary doctrines are those articulated in the

18

earliest creeds (The Apostles' Creed, the Nicene Creed, etc.), where church fathers and mothers in the first few centuries organized what the New Testament was saying about the world. They were receiving doctrines and putting them together. But consider how few these "primary" doctrines are. They are *essential*—they are worth dying over, in my opinion—but not *every* idea or doctrine is worth dying and fighting for. What those doctrines are and how to classify them is outside the scope of this book.[24] There is much more room for Christians to debate and decide for themselves while remaining inside what C.S. Lewis called, "mere Christianity." But so long as we believe the lie that Christianity *is* our ideas, our ideas will be so precious they will become an idol. When we get clear about which doctrines help us affirm who Jesus Christ is, we realize we can change our minds about a lot and still remain inside orthodoxy. This kind of freedom leads us to seek wisdom when considering the secondary and tertiary issues beneath Christianity, many of which end up dividing us when they should not.

* * *

Because Christian thinking is grounded in doctrine and not ideology, Christians do not fit into this world's ideological categories. Christians will have strange opinions that confuse cultural paradigms. When you ask us about marriage, we sound very conservative, but when you ask us about justice, we sound

---

[24] For more on this, please read Gavin Ortlund's fantastic book, *Finding the Right Hills to Die On: The Case for Theological Triage* (Crossway, 2020), especially pages 76-94.

like liberals. Then, ask us about forgiveness or grace and we sound like neither political side because all are welcome at Christ's table. We will also be free to re-articulate core doctrines of the faith as the culture shifts, not changing what we believe, but how we hold what we believe. This guarantees fury from all kinds of people.[25] But because God has shown up in Jesus Christ, and revealed himself to us as supreme, it's impossible for those who follow him to have an ideological camp. So long as we worship him and do what he says, the wider culture will never see the things we say and believe as coalescing into a neat set. It'll always be theology, not ideology.

But to act as if Jesus is not this supreme leads to all kinds of craziness. The most concerning thing I have seen recently as a pastor has not been a rise of evil, but a rise of foolishness—of not considering who Jesus is and what he has done, but instead considering any set of ideas. Perhaps the most insidious and devilish thing right now is all of those who have fully embraced evil as normal, even boring.[26] More dangerous than the one person enacting wickedness or injustice are the millions who consider it commonplace and unnoticeable.

There are certainly evil people in positions of power all over

---

[25] These examples are given and expounded upon in Larry Hurtado, *Destroyer of the gods: Early Christian Distinctiveness in the Roman World* (Baylor University Press, 2017). A study of church history and global Christianity will reveal that the gospel has offended every cultural ideology it has ever entered. It just offends different aspects, depending on the culture. In the modern West, the gospel offends in its sexual ethic and affirmation of miracles, in parts of Asia or the Middle East, the doctrine of grace and forgiveness is repugnant.

[26] The BBC documentary *Hypernormalization* by the wonderful filmmaker, Adam Curtis, is a fantastic exploration into this. Because Curtis is so anti-capitalistic, I'm pretty sure you could watch this movie on YouTube.

the world, but the truth is that none of those evildoers would be able to do much if they did not have the fools behind them, next to them, and below them, looking upon their actions without much brain activity or humility. More dangerous than a group of people with evil intentions is a group of people with no intentions at all. A mob. A gaggle of goons. Philistines with phones. No sense of culture, no contemplation or slow-thinking, no sense of empathy or curiosity, no reading list, no friends with counter opinions, no service-oriented work in their week, no resistance to their phone, no questions or critiques, no creativity or new concepts, no understanding of literature or taste in music or interest in history or integrity… just a shell with feelings in front of a screen. It's a terribly sad life and a dangerous addition to a society. Foolishness is worse than evil.

Does Christianity have anything to say about this? Does our faith allow us to "think whatever we want" and to "make up our own minds" after having "done our research?" Furthermore, are we permitted to share all of the "amazing ideas" we hear on podcasts and YouTube videos because *we* found it interesting, sitting alone on our bed? Just because something is interesting, does it mean it is right? Does what we share affect our soul? Does what we consume change us? Does God have anything to do with the streams of information we are receiving and sharing?

I am interested in all of these questions. But I am not interested in sounding alarms. Christians have always been tempted by "ideas."[27] Believers throughout the centuries have always existed within a culture of information and, therefore,

---

[27] More on this in chapter 4.

21

misinformation. Whether it was the Stoics and Cynics of first century Rome or the Jordan Peterson listeners of 2022, the followers of Jesus are never free from attractive philosophy that could (in their minds) replace their Christianity.[28] But through all of this, believers never need to be afraid. Why is this? Why, after thousands of years, has Christianity stood as various ideologies and philosophies have come and gone? When foolishness abounds, why and how can Christians remain so peaceful? This book will touch on a few of these historical and cultural examples so we might understand just how good the gospel of Jesus Christ is at destroying ideas and setting our minds free inside the "power of God and the wisdom of God" (1 Corinthians 1:24). Very little is new. No alarms necessary.

* * *

Before we move on, there are two words that will find their way into many of these chapters, whether explicitly or implicitly: *humility* and *wisdom*. While I do not pretend to know the psychological path out of the madness we're in, we may have a route theologically as we embrace how Scripture treats these two terms.

Humility is an accurate self-assessment in light of knowing God. Worship is a key to humility. Wisdom is a reverent submission to God and his ways. Knowing God is a key to wisdom. I honestly see very little of this in our modern discourse—even very little of this in churches. If we start with humility, we will use the phrase "I may be wrong" and we will

---

[28] Robert Louis Wilken, *The Christians as the Romans Saw Them,* second edition (Yale University Press, 2003), pgs. 68-93.

listen with great intention to our friends we do not understand. We will do this graciously as we sit under Christ's supremacy over all of life and all ideas. If we are people of wisdom, we will be people of worship, reverence, and careful understanding. We will be slow—especially slow to anger—and we will not be careless with our minds. As you read this book, think about those two terms—humility and wisdom—and think about how you might seek to understand how they might find a home in your life.

It is, for sure, tough to know what to do. It makes no sense to reason with some people right now because you cannot reason with the unreasonable. You cannot appeal to logic when the person is not operating out of said logic or even interested in it in the first place. This is why pastors preach so emotionally right now. It's almost as if the only way to change someone is to help them feel a type of way about God. I'm not sure that will do it. A brainless, proud believer is as dangerous as an empty-headed and arrogant pagan. Both of them will hop from speaker to speaker or pastor to pastor or writer to writer or personality to personality as they look for a satisfying emotional experience that allows them not to think. In this book, I am not asking us to abandon our convictions, but to see them and hold them differently. "Ideas" and any ideology we might serve, must be properly viewed in light of the person and work of Jesus.

How do you avoid ideological captivity? How do you talk with people who are in it? How do you make sense of conspiracy theories, strange beliefs, and stubborn heads? How do we think about our faith when everyone is sharing "ideas" for us to consider? How do you hold on to faith when everyone is crazy? And how, after all of this, can you be sure you're not?

This is my best attempt.

2

Whatever you do, do not pity the fool

"I pity the fool!"

-Mr. T

"Claiming to be wise, they became fools…"

-Romans 1:22

* * *

Only one bumper sticker has ever changed by life. This bumper sticker has since turned into a meme, but—and this is where I begin my Dad Voice—when I was young, memes were printed words that went on stickers that we then put on the backs of our cars. Many sermons used to reference such things.

This particular bumper sticker was so simple, with plain black text and a white background. It caught my eye because, unlike the common stickers expressing political leanings or specific drug preferences, this one was wordy but simple. In plain white text on a black sticker, it said this:

> "Everything happens for a reason. Sometimes that reason is you're stupid and you make bad decisions."

I cannot tell you how much this resonated with my entire experience and provided a forecast for the rest of my life. I must have been 16 when I saw it for the first time and I have thought about it often since. I have forgotten countless sermons through my life, I have forgotten names of important people, and massive events in history; I have even forgotten key moments in my own life. But I have not forgotten this bumper sticker and I will not so long as I live with a sound mind.

Why?

Because it is so deeply true. We've seen this, haven't we? The friend who comes to you complaining about their life, only to reveal details to convince you that everything they've complained about has been a result of their own actions. We know the person who has dated person after person only to ignore the common denominator in every relationship is not the other person, but them. Everyone in your friend group sees it, but they stay blind to the consequences of their own actions. This is why I would reject wholeheartedly the advice of Mr. T and warn you to, in fact, *not* pity the fool. At the same time you feel sorry for someone who is blind to his or her own foolishness, you are probably blind to yours. Foolishness is much more difficult to escape so long as we cannot escape our existence. We are all stupid and we all make bad decisions.

* * *

What does it feel like to be a fool? We know it well because we live inside the prison of our own actions. We very rarely do what we say we will do with the intention we communicate. God is the only one whose speech (communicated intention) and action (physical display) are bound up together: what God says, he does. All the time. More pointedly, what God *desires*, he says, and what he says, he does (Numbers 23:19, Psalm 115:3). Theologians often note the inseparable nature of these things—God's speech and action.[29] God's creative action in Genesis 1 is bound up in his speech. The two are one. "'Let there be light!' And there was light" (Genesis 1:3). God's creative act *is* his Word.[30] This is why the least foolish thing a human being can do is submit their entire being beneath God's wisdom.

Humans are famous for operating much differently than God by separating their intentions ("I love everyone") from their speech ("I love you") and their actions (selflessly acting in another's best interest). In the book of Genesis, after the creation account of a God whose actions and speech are inextricable, the author tells a Dostoyevskian tale of a family of fools who constantly do not do what they intend or say

---

[29] For a summary of Thomas Aquinas's thought on this and how his theology separated the God of the Bible from Greek metaphysics, see David B. Burrell, *Aquinas: God and Action* (University of Chicago Press, 2008).

[30] Augustine was one of the first theologians to present this with clarity. Writing on Genesis 1, he says, "[A]nd whatever you say must come into being comes into being; and you don't create in any way except by speaking—however, not everything you create by speaking comes into being at the same time, or is eternal." Augustine, *Confessions*, Book 11.9 (Penguin Random House, Modern Library Edition, 2017), Translated by Sarah Ruden, pg. 353.

they will. This is to say that Genesis is the story of God and idiots. Commenting on Jacob's life, the Jewish scholar Avivah Gottlieb Zornberg writes, "If Jacob had fulfilled his vow…He would have been the first human being to engage in this most alarming, glorious act of interfusing words and acts, so that each informs the other."[31] And since Jacob, there has been only one human being capable of marrying their words and their actions to perfection. Other than Jesus Christ, Son of God, the world has been ridden with idiots.[32]

Do you know the idiot? The fool? The unwise? The idiot, like Jacob (or anyone else, really), refuses to look back on his long line of missteps and see the common denominator: themselves. An idiot or a fool is the empty-brained, the dull mind, the haphazard thinker, the lame conscience. It's the parrot, the re-tweeter, the deadhead. Scrolling through their feed, the fool follows and likes the things that remind them of themselves and their own interior experience. The fool is blind, quick, and confident. Challenge is a threat to them, critical thinking is just too difficult, and worship is boring. The fool doesn't just say, "there is no God," he doesn't care to think about God in the first

---

[31] Avivah Gottlieb Zornberg, *The Beginning of Desire: Reflections on Genesis* (Schocken, 2011), p. 224-225

[32] I will use the word "idiot" a lot in this book and I suppose I can defend it here. The word "idiot" is strong, but useful, because the Hebrew term for "fool," which is used well over 100 times in Scripture, is quite harsh. Harsh terms suit the gravity of the situation and grab attention where attention is needed. The term for "fool" in the Hebrew was not lighthearted, but devastatingly sharp. For more on the Wisdom Literature's use of the word "fool," and the consequences of retribution theologies in connection to this term, see Tremper Longman III, *The Fear of the Lord is Wisdom: A Theological Introduction to Wisdom in Israel* (Baker Academic, 2017), pgs. 177-198.

place (Psalm 14:1).[33] A fool can also be so confident of who God is that they never question their presuppositions about his nature and commands (Deuteronomy 29:18-19), but he can also be the kind of person who is so certain God isn't even real (Proverbs 28:26). Idiots can be theists or atheists—whatever they are, they're sure about it. He or she only cares that they are understood and that they feel good and safe. They are dangerous. Speaking in Biblical language, to be under "ideological captivity" is to have become a fool, an idiot.

Depending on your translation, the word "fool" will appear in your Bible between 170-185 times. In Proverbs, "Lady Folly" is described as a seductress who leads you to your demise. Jesus, Paul, James, Peter, and God himself all called certain people "fools" (Matthew 23:17, Romans 1:22, James 2:20, 1 Peter 2:15, Jeremiah 4:22, just to name a few). Throughout all of Holy Scripture, we are given repeated and consistent warnings about becoming this thing called a fool and I am certain we have just as many or more falling into idiocy today as did in the time of those writings.

The reason some (definitely not all!) bad things happen in our life is because *we* are living that very life. Inside the prison of our existence (or "sin," in biblical language), we are unable to come out from under the consequences of our actions. We are helpless. For however much we can polish our intentions

---

[33] Commenting on Psalm 14:1, Augustine says, "whilst they love this world and love not God; these are the affections which corrupt the soul, and so blind it, that the fool can even say, "in his heart, There is no God." Augustine of Hippo, "Expositions on the Book of Psalms." *Saint Augustine: Expositions on the Book of Psalms*. Ed. Philip Schaff. Trans. A. Cleveland Coxe. Vol. 8. (New York: Christian Literature Company, 1888), pg. 46. A Select Library of the Nicene and Post-Nicene Fathers of the Christian Church, First Series.

before our families and friends ("I mean well!" or "my heart is in the right place!"), the truth is that these intentions are mostly self-focused and overly self-assured.[34] Many bad things follow our life and take root in our past not because a malevolent force is after us (although, in sin, there is), but often because we lack any cognitive ability to understand the gaps between our speech and our action. Even if you say you will do something and you do that thing, you will probably do it at the wrong time or in a manner that it is interpreted by another person to be bad. You and I, on our own, cannot win.

This is why Paul will write, centuries after Genesis, that humanity continually loses its footing because we *think* we are wise, but in claiming to do so, we become the very idiots we swear we are not: "Claiming to be wise, they became fools…" This is a solid summary of the human race (Romans 1:22).

* * *

One obsession of the writers of the Hebrew Bible was the human choice between wisdom and foolishness. To be wise—to not be a fool or an idiot— according to the Old Testament, is to listen and obey the word or command of God, to adhere to what God says with reverent action. To be a fool was to go contrary to this, rejecting the Lord's instruction and "be wise in your own eyes" (Proverbs 3:7). The story of Adam and Eve, as has been argued by many, is a story of choosing foolishness over wisdom.[35] "So when the woman saw that the tree was

---

[34] I usually think, *Oh I got this,* right before I do something extremely stupid.

[35] See Roland E. Murphy's *The Tree of Life: An Exploration of Biblical Wisdom Literature* (Wm. B. Eerdmans Publishing Co., Grand Rapids, 1990).

good for food, and that it was a delight to the eyes, and that the tree was to be desired to make one wise, she took of its fruit and ate" (Genesis 3:6). In its simplest form, foolishness is a decision, a decision to reject God's ways.

It is no surprise, then, to read the opening chapters of the Bible's main book of wisdom, Proverbs, and hear about the choice set before every human being: "The fear of the LORD is the beginning of knowledge; fools despise wisdom and instruction," (Proverbs 1:7) and so, the writer goes on, "Let your heart hold fast my words; keep my commandments, and live. Get wisdom; get insight; do not forget, and do not turn away from the words of my mouth" (Proverbs 4:4b-5).

Throughout Proverbs, Wisdom and Folly (foolishness) are personified as two women (Proverbs 1 and Proverbs 8-9). The call is to marry and commit fully to Lady Wisdom and reject Lady Folly. Proverbs was originally written as a kind of handbook for men to walk their sons through, so that they would understand everything from common business etiquette to mature and practical relationship advice. The entire book is full of a choices: listen and obey the voice of Wisdom, calling you to a rich life in God's presence and goodness, or do not listen, go your own way, and suffer the consequences of such actions.

> 20 Wisdom cries aloud in the street,
>   in the markets she raises her voice;
>   21 at the head of the noisy streets she cries out;
>   at the entrance of the city gates she speaks:
>   22 "How long, O simple ones, will you love being simple?

> How long will scoffers delight in their scoffing
> and fools hate knowledge?
>
> -Proverbs 1:20-22

Humans beings, like Jacob or any other family member from Genesis, reject the wisdom of God to pursue their own ideas about life. Embedded in our humanity is the belief that we have good ideas about how to live and think, that we are honest people with helpful things to say. We are, we believe, "good people," and we "understand some things" about life and parenting and finances and God and technology. At our core, "we got this," we think, and we do not believe that our actions are the prison that they actually are. This is the beginning point of our catastrophe. Everything happens for a reason. Sometimes that reason is you're stupid and you make bad decisions. We cannot escape doing the wrong thing because we constantly believe we're the right person.

If we're not good people, then are we, as some theologians and pastors have claimed, bad people? I do not believe so. Scripture speaks of sin as an infectious, alien power that "reigns" in human beings (Romans 6:12), it sits "at the door" (Genesis 4:7). When talking about his own misbehavior, Paul says, "It is no longer I who do it, *but sin* that dwells within me" (Romans 7:18, emphasis mine). We are both good people made in the image of God and bad people corrupted by sin and death, tainted by a malevolent power. It is precisely this incongruousness combined with our own self-justifying mind that leads us to a foolish life. Again, unlike God, we are a walking contradiction.

So is the natural conclusion here to simply choose wisdom constantly and experience the fullness of human life? Should we just…make better decisions? Submit to God's wisdom and his ways? Oh, if only it were so simple.

* * *

One of the marks of our own foolishness is believing in our own ingenuity. We think if we made better decisions, the world would be a better place. This is only true to a certain extent. Of course the slight changes of our moral behavior makes the world a more habitable place. But sin and foolishness are like out of tune violins in a symphony: the effects are inescapable. Western believers like me would love for everyone to believe that "sin" is a bad personal decision that reaps only bad personal consequences. That sometimes happens. But when your neighbor is out of tune, you can play all the right notes you'd like…it's still a mess. We can only change so much. Sin is a much bigger problem; foolishness does not just affect you.

Many people prize the "progress of humankind," only to just change clothes on the same body. Progress, for all that we talk about it, is a complete lie in regards to the human condition. Progress certainly happens in technology, culture, and art, but it does not happen in the human soul. This is why reading Shakespeare or Homer is an invigorating experience hundreds of years later, why movies become "classic," and why, even though jazz is a dying genre, there is nothing like listening to Bill Evans play the piano. Art, culture, and technology clothe the human soul and create a kind of reciprocation of experience: we feel these things because they express something about the human condition that is *timeless*. Great books and movies of culture only reinforce the truth that we are what we are and we will not change. Bach invokes similar feelings as Bon Iver because, at their deepest level, they are the same person, expressing differently the same fractured spirit in all of us. We are *all* not well and we cannot help ourselves. The Bible calls this "sin."

* * *

Developing humility and wisdom comes through an understanding of sin and a curiosity about our life before God. We cannot stay wise and avoid ideological captivity without the doctrine of sin. And we also cannot find wisdom if we lose careful curiosity. To avoid the doctrine of sin will be to avoid humility, thereby causing us to puff up in the pride of our own minds, quickly becoming the fools we long not to be. To reject curiosity will be to avoid wisdom, making us into overly simplistic believers who get scared of new ideas, seeing them as "threats" they most certainly are not.

We have already said that the Bible speaks of sin as an inescapable alien power, a deadly virus unleashed on a helpless creation. Sin is not just moral misdeeds—it is a power and principality, the operating force of destruction that is against God. So long as we live here, we are "under the power" of sin and its effects (John 12:31, Romans 5:12, Ephesians 2:1-3). Unless something happens. Unless Someone happens. Unless—and there just might be the chance—the Someone comes to us.

Until then, we will continue to look for the next great idea to save us. We are one podcast series away from really understanding our diet, or one book away from being inspired again at work, or one Twitter thread away from emotional stability. We scroll and search and talk and text and love and breakup and create and listen and watch all believing that something is "out there" to help us. Fools notoriously think ideas will save them. Fools are famous for thinking they have what it takes. Fools have no wisdom and no humility. But, man, do they have effort.

And sometimes effort works for a little bit. This is why your dad is listening to Joe Rogan and why your mom is obsessed with that podcaster or your friend incessantly follows that one influencer who calls themselves a writer. It's why so many Christians through the coronavirus pandemic, as they were holed up with their phones, slowly transformed out of the image of Christ and into the image of a pseudo-expert. It's why your parents changed how they talk or your friend posts super weird things now. This is curiosity masked in pride and arrogance. It is how we have become "wise in their own eyes" and, "Claiming to be wise..." become fools (Romans 1:22). Grabbing on to the latest "ideas" about society, culture, and politics, some people have turned into something far worse than we could imagine. They did not become evil; they became fools.[36]

If the answer to our quest for wisdom begins in the first person ("I think" or "I believe" or "I know" or "I read") we are hopeless. There must be another character in the story. Hope for humanity must come from outside the prison of our own beliefs and actions—and the inconsistencies between

---

[36] Another common biblical word for this issue would be "submission," a very underdeveloped subject in our public discourse. The fool's problem is not that they are not submissive, but because they are submissive to the wrong things or lack discernment for where to submit themselves. For an interesting narrative on this, read the novel *Submission* (Picador, 2016) by the controversial French novelist Michel Houellebecq.

those two things. If salvation comes from ideas, we become proud, but if salvation comes from Someone else, we are utterly humiliated in the best way possible. An invasion is necessary for us to come out from under our own idiocy. We do not need new ideas. We need something *to have happened*. We need an arrival, an interruption in our own history, a revelation from somewhere else, a Word from beyond. There is nothing—absolutely nothing—on the inside of human history and philosophy that will offer us a path out of foolishness. We are *that* helpless. Something else must come *to* us and happen *to* us...something else entirely.

3

Christianity is not an idea

"What is there, then in Christ Jesus? There is that which horrifies: the dissolution of history in history, the destruction of the structure of events within their known structure, the end of time in the order of time."

- Karl Barth, *The Epistle to the Romans*

"It is the metaphysically fundamental fact of Israel's and the church's faith that its God is freely but, just so, truly self-identified by, and so with, contingent created temporal events."

- Robert W. Jenson, *Systematic Theology*

* * *

Wehe are a culture obsessed with ideas. In order to gratify our insatiable need for more thinking — more *right thinking*, we think — we have created what we call "content." The content produced is then produced again...and again. A pompous 18-minute talk given by an expert or pseudo expert (what's the difference these days, anyway?), packaged into a "radio hour," posted as a podcast, produced as a video, transcribed as a blog...*more ideas, please*. As discussed in the previous chapter, we long for the right set of ideas to get us out of this madness.

We read an article and quickly insert into a conversation with someone who is tolerating our pontifications: "I was reading an article..." We listen to podcasts, dumping information and stories into our heads, "getting the gist of it," listening to the interview with the author to pretend we read the book. We don't just create shows anymore, but shows about shows, content for the content. All of this just to keep up with our Culture of Ideas.

Forget the primary sources, the original research, but give us the video because in there we will "get the idea," which is all we ever wanted anyway. We want the truncated version of the larger narrative, the bite-sized piece. We want what fools want: the idea.

* * *

We like ideas because we can regurgitate them. But like any regurgitating, it comes out in a disgusting manner, infected with our own bile. What was originally well-produced and interesting comes out as contaminated and awkward. When we re-present the ideas, we think we're displaying it just as clearly as the original, but in reality, it becomes an amalgamation of our beliefs, prejudices, and misunderstandings. The original idea is somewhere in there (I guess?), but it's difficult to recognize.

But down the line, after several regurgitations, we find ourselves spewing ideas that are, without question, absurd. Somewhere behind your "medical advice" is a crazy person who came up with the "original" idea. At the beginning of your "theological" idea is someone who owned a slave or killed his wife. If I could trace the primary sources and pseudo-experts of your proposed idea you've just started regurgitating (which I won't), I would most likely find the ridiculousness I *feel like* I'm hearing from you, just on clearer display. It would be a purer form of the absurd.

* * *

Enter into our world of idea-regurgitation this: well-meaning Christians who, desiring to play the game the world is playing, spout off things they heard or read this week that most aligns with their temperament. If the game is "who has the best idea," my brothers and sisters have often presented Christianity as just that: "the best idea." For them, the gospel is always "threatened" by some ideology or another: critical race theory, evolution, woke-ism, nationalism, or colonialism. They will tell you that we need to get Christianity *right* and understand its main concepts as a way to combat these "other" ideas.

These friends hope to present Christianity the same way ideas are currently presented: let's make an air-tight theory, a well-produced constructed philosophy, and then give it to the world as the superior "worldview." They see Christianity as a set of ideas on the battlefield with other ideas. Their beliefs are then repurposed inside of a perfectly crafted theological system (thank you, academia): find me a Ph.D! Let's get him/her on the record! There, inside of a cold presentation, we make ourselves something we consider beautiful: a lovely idea, fantastic content. Publish it. *Ah, we have made a beautiful thing,* we think, until we present it to the world only to realize with shock: it's no longer Christianity. It's just ideas *about* Christianity.

Suddenly we realize the regurgitation we have just performed. Our disgusting bile has reformed what was once food but is now vomit. No one in the world wants it. It's just another idea; and it sort of sounds like every other idea. We have plenty of those, why another? Our ideas for our life abound: the idea that yoga is good for me, that a concert is a transcendent experience, that a podcast keeps me informed, that a video makes me smart.

All of these are ideas about ideas. But true Christianity offers us nothing on the plane of ideas. Remember: it is a revelation of another world, an alternate kingdom. In this chapter and the next one, I want to show you precisely what Christianity is and is not. By knowing what the very nature of our faith is, it will show us its relationship to other ideas and ideologies. You'll be able to spot an ideology after having seen your faith most clearly. If Christianity is presented as such it will be received as such: another idea to compliment my life of ideas. But if we see it for what it is—the offensive yet healing revelation from heaven—we just may be saved.

* * *

Good news arrives like this: Christianity is not an idea. Christianity is an event, an assault, an invasion, a moment, a history.[37] Christianity does not give us "something to think about," but the report that something has happened — an occurrence, an event: Jesus Christ came and died and rose again. Yahweh, the God of Israel, brought the people out of Egypt. Something has happened. In the gospel, we do not respond to an idea about humanity, but an occurrence within humanity: God has arrived.

The "event" that is Christianity is the arrival of God in Christ. And this event means very little if the person at the center of the event is not who he and his followers said he was: "the fullness of deity dwelling bodily" (Colossians 2:9). The person (Jesus Christ) inside the event of Christianity makes the entire faith what it is—he and he alone is the cornerstone.

"If Christianity is a theory," writes the scholar Ben Myers, "then salvation is ultimately an intellectual matter. It is about getting rid of the wrong ideas and acquiring the right ones… The heart of Christianity is not an idea but a brute fact… not a general principle but a person with a name: Jesus…"[38] Christianity is not threatened by ideas because it is not an idea or sets of ideas. It's playing a whole different game. If anyone tells you there's a "threat" to the gospel, they are fundamentally misunderstanding the gospel.

The primary nature of the God of the Bible is not a divine being spouting ideas from heaven, but a person come into reality, a God of events, of arrivals. Building off of the work of

---

[37] "Enemy-occupied territory—that is what the world is. Christianity is the story of how the rightful king has landed, you might say landed in disguise, and is calling us all to take part in the great campaign of sabotage." C.S. Lewis, *Mere Christianity* (HaperCollins, 1980), pg. 46.

[38] Ben Myers, *The Apostles' Creed* (Lexham Press, 2018), pgs. 61–63.

Robert Jensen, Andrew Root identifies God as the God of the exodus and the God of the resurrection — that by these two events (and all the events surrounding them) we can know who God is. "This God is a living God because this God identifies with events," he writes, "making the happenings of these events God's identity. We can know who God is by spotting the events that God identifies with."[39]

And this is true. Reading your Bible is reading a story of arrivals: God coming into human history in various and mysterious forms. He is the God who comes walking in the Garden of Eden (Genesis 3:8), the God who sits and eats with Abraham (Genesis 18:8), the God who comes as flame, thunder, pillars of smoke (Exodus 3:4, 13:22, 19:18–19). He is the one who arrives in a low whisper (1 Kings 19:12), a shout (Psalm 47:5), a song (Psalm 22:3). He arrives in a womb (Luke 1:35), a stable (Luke 2:7), a hill (Matthew 5:1), a home (Mark 2:1), a court (Matthew 27:1), and a cross (Matthew 27:24). Finally, after being looked for in a grave, he arrives in a garden all over again (John 20:15).

The news given to our idea-obsessed culture is not another idea, but a question of events: *how has God come to us? How is God coming to us now? How might God be arriving today? What is God doing?* If God truly is known to us through events and not ideas, then we must assume there are things occurring in this world that are not just *about him* (like an idea), but *actually*

---

[39] Andrew Root, *The Pastor in a Secular Age* (Baker Academic, 2019), pg. 201–202

*him...*he has come...he is coming...he will come again.[40]

He told us to look for him in the eyes of the poor, the naked, the lonely, the exile, the prisoner, and the downcast (Matthew 25:31–46). He warned us his kingdom will be hidden, but precious (Matthew 13:31–33). He told us—and this is the most shocking of them all—that he could be found *here* (Deuteronomy 4:29, Jeremiah 29:13, Matthew 6:33, Luke 11:9). The alternate kingdom of heaven is coming to earth in Christ.

God must not be theorized, but actualized. So long as we consider him to be pontificated about—regurgitated as an idea—make no mistake: we will not find him. But, if we look into the eyes of those who are coming to us, if we pray with people near us, and confront the difficulties of our differences, if we look carefully beyond the stars and in front of our faces... maybe, just maybe...we will see him coming to us: his arrival. Remember the image of the sun from C.S. Lewis in chapter 1? We cannot mistake the sun for a rock we see on the ground. We now look at ideas through the experience of having seen Jesus Christ, not the other way around.

The "fool" we outlined in the last chapter can now be avoided—not by good philosophy or by having the right ideas, but by having a kind of encounter. To become "wise" is to know the "power and wisdom of God" found in the person and work of Jesus Christ (1 Corinthians 1:24). We do not reject foolishness by becoming smart. We reject foolishness by

---

[40] Low-church Christians like Evangelicals and Baptists may be unfamiliar with the "Memorial Acclamation," which is said in most Catholic, Anglican, Methodist, and Lutheran Churches: "Christ has died; Christ is risen; Christ will come again!" Sometimes sung but often simply recited, this acclamation is a truly wonderful and succinct summary of the core tenants of Christian belief. The entire utterance is affirmations of events, not ideas.

knowing the Lord Almighty and what he has done. Through the living, active, and real experience of relating with God, wisdom comes. There's no other way: "The fear or the LORD is the beginning of wisdom" (Proverbs 9:10). A Christian is not someone who knows a lot of ideas about God and faith, they are a being who has found another Being. Through the event of Jesus Christ, we come to know God himself. In our fearful worship of this Living Person, we find wisdom and reject foolishness.

Many well-meaning teachers today will tell you to be afraid of some set of ideas that will ruin your Christianity. But what if Christianity could not be ruined? What if, when our Christianity was properly understood, there could be no threat to it? What if the message and event of the cross was so profound that nothing could destroy it? What if Christianity as an event was such good news that it *surpassed* human ideas? That would be good news.

4

Christianity is stupid

"Christianity is the most ridiculous, the most absurd, and bloody religion that has ever infected the world."
-Voltaire

"The God of the philosopher is a concept derived from abstract ideas; the God of the prophets is derived from acts and events…to believe is to remember."
- Abraham Joshua Heschel, *God in Search of Man*

* * *

Inside the cities of the ancient Greco-Roman world, philosophers were extremely popular. It was a great way to make a living. You were often your own boss, making your own hours, creating your own content, and finding an audience you could build around your message. Students would pay to follow specific teachers who attached themselves to certain schools of thought. Philosophers in Rome would work hard at developing the right look, feel, and rhetoric for their base audience to respond. People would pay money to get practical advice, good stories, and general wisdom from those who positioned themselves as expert teachers. This is all to say that the philosophers of the Ancient Roman world were the first podcasters...or YouTubers...or social media influencers. It's a different age and a different technology, but it's the same racket.

"Philosophers became hucksters," writes the historian Robert Louis Wilken, they were "salesmen marketing the ideas and beliefs of their respective schools...they offered advice on how to live one's life and deal with personal problems. Appealing less to reason and logic than to emotion and feeling, philosophers appeared as traveling evangelists, directing their hearers to the wondrous accomplishments of the founder of the school, its venerable tradition, or the high regard in which many people viewed it."[41]

This is essentially a description of podcasters and social media influencers today, is it not? Not convinced? Wilken goes on: "the appeal of the philosopher frequently had less to do with the teachings of his school than with how the philosopher dressed, what kinds of success he could promise its adherents, and which philosophy was fashionable and highly regarded in influential circles."[42]

Technology has changed, but we have not. The way we get the philosophers—and even the name "philosopher"—has changed,

---

[41] Robert Louis Wilken, *The Christians as the Romans Saw Them,* second edition (Yale University Press, 2003), pg. 74.

[42] Wilken, pg. 76

but we still prioritize well-presented information above good information. We still crave wisdom for how to live from well-dressed people who speak confidently in front of a well-lit room rather than from actual experts.[43] As much as we'd *like* to read, most of us watch a video or listen to a well-produced podcast and consider ourselves "convinced."

* * *

In the 100s-200s A.D., the Christian movement was taking off rapidly in many Roman occupied territories throughout what is now Greece, Turkey, and the Middle East. All of the early cities of the Christian church—from Rome itself to cities like Smyrna, Corinth, Ephesus, and Carthage—were under the influence of "the philosophers." To say that Paul or James or Peter never dealt with ideological captives is a misread on the history these Christians were hidden within. Certainly the speed and ease of access to such things has changed, but the human proclivity towards a flat and dull mind is quite old.

The ancient Greeks chased philosophers who promised *sophia* (their word for "wisdom"). To have *sophia* was to have everything. *Sophia* was, to them, the divine knowledge, a "supreme intelligence"[44] that was unlocked through careful living and thinking. The person who had *sophia* was admirable, smart, and interesting. They had their life together and they spoke with great eloquence and confidence. This is to say that those who had *sophia* were celebrated and envied.

Most Greeks and Romans desired *sophia* more than any other

---

[43] I never trust a self-proclaimed intellectual with ripped abs...just my rule.

[44] From *Strong's Lexicon*, accessed on Logos Bible Software.

virtue. They craved being right and saying the right thing—it was a kind of salvation. Here's Leon Morris, New Testament scholar: "The Greeks were absorbed in speculative philosophy. No names were more honored among them than the names of their outstanding thinkers. From the lofty heights of their culture they looked down on and despised as barbarians all who failed to appreciate their wisdom."[45]

The Greco-Roman love of *sophia* is most talked about in Paul's letters to the Corinthian church. Here, the Christian community had their ears directed more towards popular speakers than the word of God, which led Paul to write scathingly about the difference between the two in his first few chapters of 1 Corinthians. Richard Hays, another New Testament scholar, said that "There is no reason to think that the Corinthians [Christians] were any different" from the philosophy-craven Romans and Greeks living in their city. "[The believers] were simply absorbing such attitudes from the popular philosophers and rhetoricians around them and baptizing them into Christian discourse."[46] The early church had their own misinformation problem. Human beings are always on the lookout for an expert to tell them what to think so they don't have to learn how to do it for themselves.

* * *

The world philosophy in Ancient Rome was one of privilege,

---

[45] Leon Morris, *1 Corinthians: An Introduction and Commentary.* Vol. 7. (Downers Grove, IL: InterVarsity Press, 1985).

[46] Richard Hays, *The Conversion of the Imagination: Paul as Interpreter of Israel's Scripture* (Eerdmans, 2005), pg. 20

access, and status. It was into this particular culture of ideas that the message of a Crucified Savior appeared and took major ground. Interestingly enough, "the gospel"—the good news about Jesus—does not come to humanity through wise sayings from philosophers or sophisticated rhetoric for orators and teachers. Instead it comes from a manger, from a child, and from a bloodied cross. The transformational message given to humanity is "folly" to those who do not know God or his ways (1 Corinthians 1:18).

This is Paul's great argument in perhaps one of his most eloquent passages, 1 Corinthians 1:17-2:5. Paul says that "Christ did not send me to baptize but to preach the gospel, and not with words of eloquent wisdom, lest the cross of Christ be emptied of its power" (1 Corinthians 1:17). The term "eloquent wisdom" in the Greek is the single word we've been talking about: *sophia*. Paul did not come with *sophia*; He came with a gospel. He did not come with advice, but an announcement. Later, near the end of this section he gets even more emphatic: "When I came...I did not come...with lofty speech or wisdom (*Sophia*)...but in demonstration of the Spirit and of power, that your faith might not rest in the wisdom of men but in the power of God" (1 Corinthians 2:1, 4-5).

Paul did not come with wise words and good ideas because his message was not a philosophical one. Christianity is not presented like the philosophers of Ancient Rome. It does not need to be dressed up; it does not need to sound fancy or eloquent or "effective." When the gospel is shared, people do not become merely enlightened, helped, or encouraged; they become humiliated, undone, and silenced, which is to say they become saved.

In between Paul's two comments of *how* he came ("not with

words of...wisdom" and "in weakness," 1 Corinthians 1:17, 2:1-5), he writes about *what he came with*—his message. Paul understood the good news of Jesus to be "a stumbling block" for Jewish people and "foolishness" to the Sophia-obsessed Greeks (1 Corinthians 1:23).

I have always loved this Greek word for "stumbling block," used in verse 23. It is *skandalon,* which is one etymological root for our word "scandal." Lenski suggests most English translations are too weak with it ("stumbling block" or "offense") and suggests, "deathtrap."[47] It's more than a scandal or an offensive thing to say. It's impossible, un-thinkable, stupid-to-consider. The Greeks thought Christianity was ridiculous, elementary, thick-headed to believe—that a cross could be an instrument through which God saves people seemed dumb.[48]

To many hearers, "the word of the cross" (1 Cor. 1:18) sounds insane: a first century rabbi is executed for the salvation of all people who believe? They don't have to do anything? There's no "application" here? What are my "next steps" with this information? But it's not "information" exactly—or at least not the information we want to hear. We want something *practical,* something we can identify and something we can change. We want to *do* it! The gospel often sounds like the opposite of

---

[47] R. C. H. Lenski, *The Interpretation of St. Paul's First and Second Epistles to the Corinthians* (Augsburg, 1963).

[48] The most compelling and masterful study of the cross in modern history was done by Fleming Rutledge in her book, *The Crucifixion: Understanding the Death of Jesus Christ* (Eerdmans, 2016), see especially her conclusions on pgs. 571-575 about the implications of the Greek term *skandalon*: "Anyone seeking to understand the cross of Christ must face certain frustrations...As this tapestry of images and motifs shows, its riches are humanly unfathomable and there is no single way of understanding it."

wisdom: someone died for you and will save and raise you. This is because grace sounds stupid to people obsessed with achieving their own identity through action items and "atomic habits." Paul was telling this church in Corinth: some people will hear this Jesus stuff and scoff. They will think the whole thing is just...well, stupid.

* * *

Christianity is not a good idea. This is because, as I have contended, it's not an idea at all. It's an event. A Word. An announcement upon humankind: Christ has come and died and risen. And this announcement is certainly something no human being would ever make up.[49] God saves through this very weakness and mystery. The "power and wisdom of God" is not a political ruler, a set of ideas, or a "way of living." It is "Christ crucified" (1 Cor. 1:23). What is God like? How might we live in this world? What kind of things should we care about? How should we love and live while on this earth? We look at the cross and allow it to shape our lives into its very form. We look at the cross and repent. We hear the good news and receive a humble heart that changes us. Paul goes on:

> "God chose what is foolish in the world to shame the
> wise; God chose what is weak in the world to shame
> the strong; God chose what is low and despised in the
> world, even the things that are not, to bring to nothing
> things that are, so that no human being might boast

---

[49] "[O]ne of the reasons I believe Christianity...is [that it is] a religion you could not have guessed." C.S. Lewis, *Mere Christianity* (HarperOne, 1980), pg. 41.

in the presence of God."

-1 Corinthians 1:28-29

The whole point of the cross is to shape you and me into the humility Christ exemplified upon it. This is how we are transformed: by staring at and contemplating the reality of Jesus Christ crucified. This "cruciforms" us into the image of humble, dying-to-self kinds of people.[50] Paul actually believes that if we contemplate the power of the cross, we will change. "Set your mind on things above...where Christ is," he says (Colossians 3:1). "Have this mind among you, which is yours in Christ" he writes elsewhere (Philippians 2:5). When we "behold" Jesus, he says, we "are being transformed into the same image" (2 Corinthians 3:18). Many teachers and Christian thinkers will try all they can to make Christianity all about something else—something it is not. They will write books, tweet, make videos, all to try to lead us away from the one thing we're supposed to do: worship. It's strange how far many "Christian" leaders will go to have you *not* think about the cross.

There is a kind of Christianity being presented right now that asks us to play by the rules of the world. These preachers and writers tell you that you need to fight the "ideas of the world" with the "ideas of God." They present Jesus as the great philosopher, as someone whose rhetoric and teaching will save you if you just practice it—instead of embracing his cross. Spiritual disciplines, to these teachers, are all about

---

[50] "Cruciformity" is a helpful theological term that I spell out right here. I am indebted to Michael Gorman, *Cruciformity: Paul's Narrative Spirituality of the Cross* (Wm. B. Eerdmans, 2001). This is certainly an academic book, but Gorman is a very accessible writer and one of my favorite Pauline scholars alive.

51

self-improvement ("they work," some of these teachers will say) and the way to experience Christianity is through the ideas presented in the Bible, and not the revelation of Jesus Christ which permeate its pages. All of this sounds great the same way a podcast sounds great and the same way an Ancient Roman philosopher sounded great to those who first heard 1 Corinthians read aloud to them at a house church gathering in the year 63 A.D. It sounds good because it sounds like us. It sounds like something *we* would come up with because it's certainly something we can hear and go do: ideas for right living, optimizing our spiritual experiencing, setting goals for spiritual improvement, utilizing spiritual disciplines for a more peaceful life.

Don't get me wrong, all of this will take you somewhere and a lot of it will work for a good amount of time. But none of it will save you from yourself. There is no salvation in spiritual ideas. None of this will allow you to feel free when you fail or hopeful when you're broken or good when you've been repugnant. If the disciplines exist to make us better they are not the spiritual disciplines of Christian history. Fasting, Scripture reading, prayer, alms giving, and everything else are embraced for the sole purpose of bringing our heart into submission to Jesus, to remind us of him and his grace. The disciplines do not remind us how good we are, they remind us how desperate we are for grace. Only the cross can save us. Only the God of Heaven breaking for us will ever show us two things we rarely believe: the depths of our own disgrace and the heights of God's incalculable mercy. It is only when we see both of these next to each other that we can actually let go of ourselves. It is only at the end of our ideas and thoughts about improving our own existence that we find God's love.

So long as you can achieve Christianity through your own mental acuity or religious performance, it is not the Christianity of Christ. The contentedness with which most of us live is all inside the realm of good vibes, interesting ideas, and "thought provoking" discussions. But none of this humbles you to the point of desperation. In fact, it usually does the opposite. Make no mistake: God comes in Jesus "so that no human being might boast" (1 Corinthians 1:30). The purest reaction to the Christian message is humility. We do not hear this good news of the cross and puff our chest; we hear the Word and fall down.

If our Christianity makes us more certain we are right, more angry at people who are "wrong," and more upset at the surrounding circumstances, then I'm not sure it's Christianity at all. A key question we might need to ask—and more importantly, one we must answer honestly—is this: does the Christianity we practice lead me to worship and grow me in humility? Have I become a more "cross-shaped" person? After having followed Jesus, am I more comfortable in my sufferings, more patient in trials, and more prayerful and loving to people close to me in daily life? Many Christians are hoping their faith will make them a more well-rounded, interesting person. They want it to work for them, to have it be a "value add" to their life. But this is not what Christianity promises. Instead, it is promised we will receive deeper, perhaps more dangerous things: righteousness, self-sacrificing love, sanctification, and redemption...all of which lead us to forget ourselves inside the complete awe of God.

Don't believe me? Near the end of the section I've been discussing in 1 Corinthians 1, Paul says that all of this is truly available to us: "Because of [Jesus] you are in Christ... who became to us wisdom from God, righteousness and sanctification and redemption, so that, as it is written, 'Let the one who boasts, boast in the Lord."

5

You are not what you think

"Californians invented the concept of life-style. This alone warrants their doom."
                                    -Don DeLillo, *White Noise*

"...man cannot tell the whole truth about himself, even if convinced that what he wrote would never be seen by others."
-Mark Twain, 1899 interview with the *London Times*

* * *

I f the cross of Jesus Christ is to shape our identity, what will that process be like? What does it look like for us to properly identify our life with the life of Christ and his cross? What does it look like to gain our life after having lost it to him? And how can we be sure we've done that? How will we know we are "cross-shaped" and not shaped by various ideas that have been slung into our headphone or our phone screens?

To answer these very important questions, we will employ a term I have heard endlessly around Christian circles since I became one twenty years ago: *identity*.

Have you heard endless sermons and worship songs and devotionals about "your identity in Christ?" Have you heard that you are "not living out of your true identity?" Have you, by chance, been instructed to "know your worth" or "to know who you are?"

If you've heard this, I imagine you've also sung songs with lyrics like these:

> *"I am who you say I am"*
> *"I am a child of God"*
> *"I am chosen"*
> *"I am yours"*

I have no qualms with these songs—I actually love them. But I think they reveal more about culture than theology, and more about how we humans *think* identity is formed than how it actually manifests in our lives.

* * *

What these songs have in common with culture is simple: we believe we are who we are (our identity) because of the ideas we posses. This is why we call ourselves "feminists" or "conservatives" or "liberals." We say we are "creative" and we say we are "scientifically-minded" because, as a culture, we use ideas to tell people who we are.

Introduce the word "Christian" to this culture and you'll see what I mean: to identify yourself as Christian, we think, is to identify ourselves to a set of ideas.

We do this because we assert that what we *think* creates who we are. We also believe that the more we announce these ideas the more people will see us as such. Just look at our social media biographies, where many of us profess our core ideas about our identity: "radical conservative" or "Christian socialist" signals to people something about who we are, but its root is in ideas we have adopted. We think the ideas we ascribe to creates our identity. But do they?

It's quite common for me to be in a conversation where people flatly say things they believe to be true about themselves that absolutely are not. A person I have experienced as highly sensitive will say, "I have thick skin." Or someone who lacks discernment says "I don't trust people very easily." I hear people who are constantly stirring up drama over small, petty things say, "I like to keep focused on the big picture—no drama." I have realized how little people actually understand themselves, and how little I understand myself too, as I am guilty of the same misjudgments. It's like how everyone who's been out of high school for seven years or more says, "I was friends with everyone in high school; I didn't really stick to one group. I was friends with jocks and goths!" As you experience them you can't help but think: *there's no way that's true.*[51]

What we say about ourselves is not always true. We are not the best at self-professing our identity, even if we love doing it. We struggle because we're deceitful and self-contradictory, but also because we're fools. We do not know ourselves that well. Secondly, the things we believe do not always make their way into our actual life. The ideas we have about ourselves ("I'm compassionate") rarely manifest as actions that define our character (serving those in need). Both Christians and non-Christians believe a lot of things that do not manifest into behavior. The Golden Rule is a good rule, but have we practiced that so consistently that it has become who we are? It's one thing to tell people who we are, it's another thing for them to tell us who we *really* are. True identity cannot be a project we do ourselves.[52]

* * *

And so what does define us? If we aren't the best judge, who is? In the previous chapters, I argued God is best known not by the

---

[51] This is why Nick Hornby's novel, *High Fidelity*, might be comforting, as he asserts in it that what you are like is not as important as what you like. Strange how I've been able to be quite friendly with the people who have great taste in music. They can be selfish and weird, but if they can talk about CCR's 2am set at Woodstock '69, or Barbara Lynn's guitar playing style, or Dave Van Ronk's B-sides, or Bobby Powell's undiscovered talent, I'll be their friend forever.

[52] The most succinct account of the failed cultural project of self-identifying our identity was done by Tim Keller in 2015 at Wheaton College. He did it in 36 minutes. See online: Tim Keller, "Our Identity: The Christian Alternative to Late Modernity's Story (11/11/2015)" found on YouTube: https://www.youtube.com/watch?v=Ehw87PqTwKw

ideas we create about him, but the events he manifested himself in: God is best known through his arrivals in our history, first of which being the cross. If this is true of him, consider this about human beings: *could it be that our identity is less formed through ideas, but through events? Could it be that we are not who we are because of what we think and believe, but we are who we are because something has occurred in our life?*

Now think about those incidental liars I spoke of earlier—those of us who make lofty suggestions about our nature that is not true ("I'm a no-nonsense person!" or "I value my family"). While these statements are not always trustworthy, there's something I've learned that is fool proof: when people start telling me their life story. When people stop telling me *who* they are and start telling me *where* they came from, I start to know that person much, much better.[53]

Of course anyone telling any story creates problems of its own because we're not the best reporters of what has happened to us. Nevertheless, the way in which people tell me the events of their life tells me far more about who that person is than if they were to tell me what they believe. The person talking to me *is that person* not because of what they think, but because of *what has happened* to them. If you tell me about your battle with cancer, or your neglectful parents, or if you tell me about the time your brother came out of the closet, or how you met your wife, got your first kiss, your first adult job, etc...I will know so much more about you than if you tell me what you "believe in." The central question of identity is not "what do you believe?"

---

[53] One of my favorite questions to ask is, "Who are your parents?" To hear someone talk about their mom and/or dad is to hear so much about that person. You can also ask people about their grandparents for bonus points.

but rather "what has happened to you?"

Andrew Root argues that major events in our lives "are written into us so deeply that they become history…shaped as the narratives of our identity (who we are)…these moments aren't just causative points in time but are events that deliver a transformation."[54] Who you were *before* the divorce or the birth or the death or the illness or the bullying is vastly different than who you are now. Events, not beliefs, are foundational to our identity.

* * *

And it is right here when I finally realize why Christ came as a man, living a life, enacting salvation inside history instead of in a philosophical text. He never wrote a book. His teachings take up a good chunk of his life story, but it's *what happened to him* (the virgin birth, the miracles, the cross, the resurrection) that's most central to his identity as the Messiah. Likewise I now see why Paul seems to be obsessive over his own personal testimony, sharing his story in various letters and repeating it through the book of Acts (Acts 9:3–8, 22:3–21, 26:12–32, Galatians 1:11–2:1–10, Philippians 3:2–10). The most important thing about Paul is not what he *thought* but what he *experienced*. Something happened to him, and if you did not know about the event, you could not know him as a person.

Taking a step forward (and to simultaneously go back to those worship songs), maybe the most important thing about us is not what we think about ourselves in light of our ideas about God ("If God is a Father, therefore I am his child"), but the

---

[54] Andrew Root, *The Pastor in a Secular Age* (Baker Academic, 2019), pg. 178

events wherein God has met us ("Christ died and rose for us" or "God has adopted me"). This means some of those songs with those lyrics do not mean less, but more, if we understand them through this paradigm: our identity is not achieved through thinking, but received through the event of the gospel.[55] Where God showed up and *how* he showed up and during what time in our life tells us so much about our identity in him.

I look for this when I hear people tell me their stories. A Christian is not a person who has good ideas about God and good ideas about themselves. A Christian is not a person with heightened self-awareness or great descriptions of their identity. A Christian is a person who has met Jesus Christ—and what is a meeting but an event? The essential characteristic of a Christian is someone who has encountered the living God and was humbled (and is continually humbled) by their encounter with the gospel. It is someone who had something happen to them. Something occurred, something changed—something outside of our control, even outside of our world.

This is why the conversion stories in the Bible vary: "salvation" is pronounced on to Zacchaeus after he declares a financial restructuring of his life, and it is also pronounced upon Saul after he renounces persecutions practices. These are both very different events. But what happened to both men? They met with Christ. They encountered the living God. An event or a series of events changed the trajectory of their life and therefore altered their identity. They became a new person after experiencing God in an event (or many events).

---

[55] The "achieved" and "received" wording is all Tim Keller. He says this a lot, but most succinctly in this clip from The Gospel Coalition: "Tim Keller: What is your identity?" Accessed March 31, 2022: https://www.youtube.com/watch?v=A1jHQE3YmPU

Fascinating, then, that we Christians can talk endlessly about *how* we became a Christian, but few of us can articulate *why* we became one. This is a beautiful thing. In fact, I'm skeptical of those who tell me they know why they first became a Christian. I'm perplexed by those who put "all the world religions" side-by-side and made some kind of intellectual ascent and "chose" Christianity. I think, *That's great, but has anything occurred in your life? Did something happen to you?* Christianity is not something of our choosing, but Someone who has chosen us. We can talk about why we are a Christian *now*, but why did we become a Christian *in the first place?* A beautiful answer to this question is a shrug of the shoulders: all we know is something happened to us. Christ came. God showed up. Grace appeared. Faith, remember, is a gift (Ephesians 2:8).

* * *

When the people of Israel were forming their national identity, it was not around principles, but events. Over and over again, Moses reminds them that they are the people God rescued from Egypt (Deuteronomy 4:34-35). That's *who they are*. They are not anything other than the ones who had something happen to them (Deuteronomy 9:6-12). To this day, God's arrival defines their collective life.

And the same is true today of the Church. The Church is not those who agree with each other about ideas (we would be doomed if this were true), but those who have experienced the resounding effects of an event upon their life. The resurrection of Jesus Christ—his living and abiding presence and power—*came upon us*. This is our identity: we are those for whom Christ died and the ones to whom the Spirit has been given. These are passive sentences because, as we have said, Christianity is not to be achieved, but received. Our mission is not to have everyone share our ideas about our identity, but for all people everywhere to share in the reception of the power of the resurrection of the Son of God.

To intellectually ascend to God or agree with God does not make you a Christian. This would be inconsequential and place you only in the company of demons and religious people (James 2:9, Matthew 22:29). No, God arrives into your life and your life is forever defined by the event or events of your conversion. It's not always dramatic, and it might be very slow, but over the course of that history, you tell the story of God's coming to you, your own redemption. It's not that you've found God, it's that he has found you, and you have been unable to escape his kindness ever since. These events define you—they redefine you—and create in you new spaces for courage, generosity, and faithfulness.[56]

In his book, *Miracles*, C.S. Lewis points out the common religious person's view of God: they make him like "a book on

---

[56] The most fascinating application of this truth is connected to those with dementia and other brain diseases. Consider people who "lose their minds" and who are described as "not themselves anymore" because of some significant cognitive illness. We often treat those with Alzheimer's or other various mental disabilities with a level of distance and apathy. People who do not know where they are or who they are seem to lose identity in Western societies. This is a weakness of the American model of identity-making: how can you *be* someone when you do not know who you are or who anyone is? Christian theology offers a profound answer: you are not who *you* say you are, but who God has said you are in Christ: you are his image, his redeemed, his child. This makes those with dementia just as valuable as those without the disease. A compelling case for personhood and human rights is found in Christian identity-making. For more see John Swinton, *Dementia: Living in the Memories of God* (Eerdmans, 2012), pgs. 153-185.

a shelf." This "god" demands nothing and does not pursue you. So long as we keep him at a distance, nothing changes about us and our world. He's just an idea. This is the god of our own thinking and therefore making. If he sits atop a shelf, he will never affect our history, our life. He will simply be thought of and discussed and studied and sung about, but never alive, never dangerous. We want to create a god who does not invade us, pursue us, or make things personal. Lewis goes on:

> "An 'impersonal God'—well and good. A subjective God of beauty, truth and goodness, inside our own heads—better still. A formless life-force surging through us, a vast power which we can tap—best of all. But God Himself, alive, pulling at the other end of the cord, perhaps approaching at infinite speed, the hunter, king, husband—that is quite another matter. There comes a hush suddenly: was that a real footstep in the hall? There comes a moment when people who have been dabbling in religion ('Man's search for God'!) suddenly draw back. Supposing we really found Him? We never meant it to come to that! Worse still, supposing He had found us?"[57]

If God is defined by his events in history, and we are defined by his personal arrivals in our own life, then the ideas we either embrace or reject have only a fraction to do with our Christianity. If ideas do not primarily define us, we are free to hold them loosely, albeit carefully. If we actually believe

---

[57] C.S. Lewis, *Miracles* (Harper Collins, 1996), pg. 150

that "Jesus alone" saves us, then any idea we have about life, art, politics, or culture can be up for discussion. Obviously, these ideas have tremendous consequences, and our thoughtful acceptance or denial of them is of great importance. They can shape much of our life for better or for worse—they just cannot do nearly as much as we think (or are told) they can. So long as we remain wise and humble before Christ, our ideas will not define us. If there is, in fact, any idea that is *actually* a "threat," it is being told that ideas can save you or define you. If you buy that, you'll find yourself defined by things that were never meant to define you and distracted from the One who actually does. Many Christians today are more profoundly shaped by their personal opinions than by the Event, the crucifixion and resurrection of Jesus Christ.

The real question at the bottom of this chapter is simple: is God personal and does he act inside human experience? If he does, then he must be related with as a *being* and not an idea. Secondly, all of our ideas about life must flow from a real, living relationship with this God, and not the other way around. Our ideas matter, but they are affected—interrupted, disturbed even—by the living reality of God's presence that collides with our life. A secret space of fellowship with God's Holy Spirit—the Living Presence of the Holy One—is the place from which and in which all of our ideas about life are formed. We think what we think and change what we think in light of knowing the Living One.

This space—often called "a relationship with God"—is securely protected and cannot be "under threat" because we did not create it and we are not its primary contributor.[58] Rather, we are "hidden with Christ in God," able to now simply "set our minds" on this true, protected reality (Colossians 3:1-3). Christians have the most freedom to be wrong and explore all kinds of ideas because it is not our ideas that save us (see the previous chapter) or define us (that's this chapter). It is the Holy One, alive and aflame, who has secured us our position in him. Nothing changes this. The only thing left vulnerable, then, is our ability to believe on the truth of this Event. We need not be afraid of ideologies, but we do need to be aware of them. Imprisoning yourself in a way of thinking is more tempting than you might think.

---

[58] Although we make *plenty* of contributions, God is the one who begins, sustains, and completes our life with him. For my thoughts on our contributions to our walk with God, see Chris Nye, *Distant God: Why He Feels Far Away...And What We Can Do About It* (Moody Publishers, 2016).

6

Your ideology is showing

"'The language of poetry is the exact opposite of the language of mass media,' I said, meaninglessly."
   -Ben Lerner, *Leaving the Atocha Station*

* * *

I want to take one, brief chapter to sit with this word "ideology." Sometimes certain words get into the stream of thinking, news making, and posting so consistently that it seems as if you hear it every minute of your day. The global pandemic has caused me to feel nauseous when reading sentences that include "unprecedented" or "the new normal." Now, "ideology" has become one of those words. Here's how it's been used in just the past two hours on Twitter (as I'm writing this):

Racist ideology

Pro-slavery ideology
Prepackaged ideology
Terf Ideology
Communist ideology
Radical ideology
Ideology of law enforcement

And that's just in the last couple of hours.

As I've said, an ideology is a system of ideas that is based in a kind of theory. It means an organized set of beliefs — the multiplication of ideas off of one big idea — a sort of family of dogmas that, while all interrelated, also are distinct and different like siblings or cousins in a family: they are different, but they share DNA. Ideologies are real and can be dangerous. Some of the ideologies mentioned in my list above led to massive amounts of suffering for millions of people. To say, as I have in this book, that Christianity is not an ideology and actually corrects our ideologies, is not to say ideologies are unimportant or that they cause no damage.

But hidden within the current *usage* of the term "ideology," I see two huge problems and one massive blind spot. We will look at the problems first, and the blind spot at the end. Quick note before I move on: this is not a chapter arguing to *never* use the term "ideology," but rather a *caution about how we use the term,* before we move on and use it all the time. Going back to the two key terms in chapter one—humility and wisdom—I desire for us to stay humble and wise in using the word "ideology," especially as I see it used (mostly incorrectly and abrasively) every second on Twitter.[59]

Problem #1: The term "ideology" paints broad strokes.

Looking at the list I collected above, do you think that systems of thinking are this simple? Is all "communist ideology" strictly the same? What about "law enforcement ideology?" Take it from me, a pastor who has been accused of possessing all kinds of "Christian ideology." When I'm told I possess a "Christian ideology" or even an "American Christian ideology," do you know what I say in reply? "Which one?"

Christian ideology — even American Christian ideology — is massively diverse and no one is like the other. Taking into consideration denomination, history, location, ethnicity, local church or...I could go on...I think I could build 100 different "Christian ideologies," and probably even more "Evangelical Christian ideologies." The same is true with most things labeled this way.

When I hear and read people use this term, I often think it's a convenient and lazy way to overly simplify a rather complex history of ideas behind something with which they disagree. Many use this term as a way to loft a grenade at something they refuse to understand in a more nuanced way. When you can categorize thousands of years of complexity with a simple term like "ideology," and then use that term to demonize your opponent, you've found your route out of a dialogue and into a

---

[59] Of course I will not argue to *never* use this term because, well, I'm using that term all over this book. I wrote this (originally) as a brief article on my Medium page in 2020, and it just was too important to not include. Take this as a kind of aside from the chapters to qualify this term appropriately.

boring monologue and probably a nauseating Twitter thread that gets you the retweets your monkey brain craves.

Problem #2: An "ideology" lacks accountability of the individual and makes you look superior.

If we accuse each other of holding "ideologies," we will never really engage with someone's *actual* ideas or beliefs. If one thought is tied to a system of thoughts that we automatically believe we fully understand, we can quickly excuse people from a minor piece of their thinking that needs to be corrected and do what we've been longing to do: write them off. Additionally, by using this term we unknowingly elevate ourselves as those who understand the entire picture — we see "the whole thing," can "take it all in" — as the rest of the peasants just "don't understand" the structure and history of ideas. It's a good move for a jerk, an even better move for a low-level troll.

Instead of telling people they're promoting this or that ideology, why don't you just say, "I think you're wrong," or, "I'm not sure that's entirely correct," or, ask a good question like, "What makes you say that?" These questions drive at the person's ability to articulate what *they* mean, instead of *you* articulating what they mean for them by subsequently categorizing them into a set of ideas that's probably too vague and disorganized to begin with.

While these two problems are certainly important, there's one massive blind spot I think we're missing when we talk about ideologies...

The blind spot: Ideologies are primarily spiritual, not intellectual.

While ideologies and discussions about them are had at the intellectual level, the Christian views them as anything but purely a game of the mind. *Ideologies have a spiritual side.* Behind any system of ideas is a long history of ideas that has been mostly shaped by influences, culture, and politics. But the ability to be *captured* by an ideology—or even for an ideology to be organized and named—is certainly something far beyond anything of this world.

It's interesting as I think on this, the number of Scripture passages that arise in my brain, but none more than this one (which was quoted at the top of this book):

> See to it that no one takes you captive by philosophy and empty deceit, according to human tradition, according to the elemental spirits of the world, and not according to Christ.
>
> -Colossians 2:8

Paul explains to this church that you can be taken "captive" by a way of thinking ("philosophy") and that this kind of philosophy can be from either or both "human tradition" and "the elemental spirits of the world." Perhaps ideologies are formed through both. The wickedness and injustice we experience works *both* with "human tradition" (history) and "elemental spirits" (demonic forces). It would certainly be well within the Biblical witness to say so.

Ideologies do not form by accident, but they are also so

pervasive and so complicated that it seems to be architected by something much worse and much more powerful than a human being or several human beings. Taking into consideration all the atrocities from certain ideologies, it seems simultaneously as if they could have never been planned *and* that they *must have been planned.* Ideologies seem to be authored by something much more ominous than a human being. But then, after being sold to our flesh, the human beings continue to, over and over again, promote and fall captive to the demonic ideology that was never meant for them in the first place. As the "human tradition" and the "elemental spirits of this world" work together, horror is unleashed (More to come in later chapters on this).

It's right here that I need to say that while you may find this strange, nearly three fourths of the rest of the world does not. White Western secular people have a lot of trouble with the demonic (and the angelic, for that matter), with the reality that we may perhaps not only be living in a world with an invisible virus, but also an invisible force of spiritual proportions that seeks only for our demise. To you who has trouble with this I might simply say, consider you might be wrong and 3/4 of the world might be right. Many cultures have no problem believing we are coexisting with intense spiritual forces. Maybe that's because it's true?

Ideologies are real, but they are not as simple as we think they are. The power to fall captive to pre-set and organized ideas has spiritual underpinnings to it and gives us every reason to be prideful. When we adopt an ideology, we also are adopted into the community who also believes that ideology, thereby making us "in the right" along with the rest of our camp.

* * *

The Church has absolutely fallen prey to this. As we have seen in just the last five years, various pastors and spiritual thought leaders have become empty echo chambers of ideologies.[60] Christians can be "taken captive," which is exactly why the New Testament repeatedly warns us of it (Ephesians 5:6, Colossians 2:8, 20, 1 Timothy 1:6-7, 6:20, 2 Timothy 4:3). As discussed in the last chapter, the primary lie—the gateway into ideological insanity—is to believe that ideas are more powerful than God, and that having the right ideas justifies your place with him. When we believe the lie that we are not "hidden with Christ," we will believe anything. To be under this ideological captivity is a spiritual kind of oppression that is absolutely available to believers. We can certainly fall. Just as much as I have argued for a kind of humility in light of the cross (chapters 1-5), we now must turn our attention to the pursuit of wisdom and the rejection of foolishness.

---

[60] I'd *love* to go down a rabbit trail of examples, but that would be a bit much and probably divisive and certainly self-serving. Let's just say here that if your pastor sounds like the internet more than the Bible, you might have yourself a problem.

7

An idiot is worse than a villain

"D.B. Cooper…should be a villain. But that overlooks the one intangible that makes Americans forgive everything else: superhuman self-assurance."

-Chuck Klosterman, *I Wear the Black Hat*

"I said that I thought most of us didn't know how truly good or truly bad we were, and most of us would never be sufficiently tested to find out."

-Rachel Cusk, *Outline*

* * *

Dietrich Bonhoeffer is frequently misrepresented as a simple man: he saw the evil of Hitler, stood against him, and was killed for it. This picture is not entirely wrong, but it is certainly incomplete. One must only read *Letters and Papers from Prison*, the posthumously published collection of writings, to see the conflicted conscience behind this pastor's actions (and inactions). The "letters and papers" are wonderful, and they include the pastor stretching his mind through short stories, theological essays, sermons, plays, and poems. Reading *Letters and Papers* is an incredible gift now in 2022 as it displays Bonhoeffer's interior deliberations—his large, open mind that led him towards the actions for which he is most remembered. These interior deliberations are what we most commonly omit from the hagiographies that surround his witness. It was not Bonhoeffer's certitude that served him best, but his lack of it.

I say that reading *Letters and Papers* is valuable for 2022 for various reasons, including but not limited to the Big Three (pandemic, racial injustice, the 2020 election), but also the tone of speaking that we take when we discuss, well, *anything* today. Online or in person, I see us projecting a kind of intellectual bravado that Bonhoeffer would most certainly find puzzling, if not wicked. All across the ideological spectrum, everyone seems quite certain of their own opinions: first, we all posited ourselves as public health experts ("I've followed the data on COVID-19 closely..." led my eyes to roll out of my head), then scholars of the civil rights struggle (A 20 year-old tweets that "MLK Jr. clearly did not support violent protests" and I immediately cremate my phone), then all of a sudden we're experts on the electoral college ("Maricopa County is an easy win for Biden" says a Best Buy employee who went to Phoenix once when he was seven).

To be certain about everything is almost always proof of our own idiocy. And yet here we are, lobbing our "certainties" into the vacuum of various digital environments only to realize we were, and are, wrong. In his *Letters,* particularly in the opening essay, "After Ten Years," Bonhoeffer will lead us through not the classic "battle" of certain evil versus certain good, but into what he believed lay beneath such a war: the struggle of wisdom versus folly.

* * *

"After Ten Years" is the essay of scattered reflections from Bonhoeffer on a decade of rising fascism. He explains how the German people lacked what he called "responsible living," and, in his view, either lapsed into a kind of "ineffectiveness," paralyzed due to a desire "to do justice on all sides," or fired up into "fanaticism," whereby the individual or group adopts "single-minded principles," they avoid any kind of discernment and go about recklessly denouncing evil without understanding why it was happening or doing anything about it.

Is this starting to sound familiar?

Additionally, Bonhoeffer critiques the German with a "conscience" that oscillates back and forth trying to land on an ethical position or politic that is air tight. Then, he criticizes those who value their "freedom" to do whatever they desire (even as the world burns) and those who prize a kind of mythic "virtue" that will never come to any moral action in civilization. *Again, is this ringing any bells?*

"Who stands fast?" Bonhoeffer asks, "Where are these responsible people?" This might be the thesis of his essay, if there is one: what does a responsible life look like in a time of chaos?

It's always easier, Bonhoeffer believed, to make "responsible living" a "principle" to discuss or an issue to resolve. Rather than seeing the world as various sets of principles to adopt or reject, Bonhoeffer sees life as areas of responsibility in which we must act. This means our opinions about events have less importance (who should be president, women's role in the church, how we should behave in a pandemic, parenting strategies, what kind of foreign policy is best, etc.) than the arenas of our possible moral action (voting, our job performance, protesting or not, how we behave at home, etc).

Our opinions certainly affect how we live, but many of the opinions and ideas we hold about life are not directly connected to our personal realms of responsibility. Ironically, the very opinions we often hold so passionately (that have no direct affect on our day-to-day life) end up affecting our life because of how firmly we hold them. I am not arguing we abandon our convictions; I am arguing that we should hold them differently. Of course, arriving at such a life of personal responsibility and a loose grip on opinions has its enemies.

* * *

The enemies of living responsibly and wisely are surprisingly not "good and evil" to Bonhoeffer. No, the primary enemy is "folly," he says. More dangerous than a "scoundrel" who enacts evil is the fool who has been duped by dangerous and asinine thinking: "Against folly we have no defense," he writes,

> "Neither protests nor force can touch it; reasoning is no use; facts that contradict personal prejudices can simply be disbelieved — indeed, the fool can counter by criticizing them, and if they are undeniable, they can just be pushed aside as trivial exceptions. So the fool, as distinct from the scoundrel, is completely self-

satisfied..."[61]

Bonhoeffer's concern for the foolishness in society mirrors my own pastoral concerns today. As conspiracy theories abound both in and outside of the church right alongside the deluge of misinformation that passes through our timelines, we have all the data in the world without any sense of wisdom, any idea for how to sort through what we cannot help but receive through news alerts, push notifications, and frantic texts from our politically minded yet existentially adrift friends. For as much as the left is concerned about justice issues that various political figures seem to ignore, or how much the right is concerned for religious liberty, they both miss the essential nature of a fool: he or she is self-satisfied, immovable, unyielding. Protests, marches, and boycotts are for the purposes of pushing back evil (and necessary, Bonhoeffer would say), but right now we are fighting something far worse than evil; we're fighting folly.

Evil, for example, withholds and suppresses certain rights; folly simply ignores them. Folly, to Bonhoeffer, means that "men are deprived of their independent judgment," they "give up trying to assess the new state of affairs for themselves." You, perhaps, have seen videos of those on one political side or another as they are shown evidence of doctored videos they once promoted as truth — the evidence is before their very eyes and, as they watch their own theories upended, they remain unmoved in their understanding of the national moment. The "Libs still suck" or the GOP are still "liars," or "the media" can't be trusted (public service announcement: there is no "the media,"

---

[61] All quotes from this chapter are from Dietrich Bonhoeffer, *Letters and Papers from Prison* (Touchstone, 1997), pgs. 1-31, unless otherwise noted.

but carry on), no matter what they have seen. Even as they witnessed on video their own side sowing deceit, they refuse to think independently about its effect on their conscience or the nation's behaviors. These people are not "evil" per se, again, they're much worse: they're idiots. And, my dear reader, if you find this section offensive or "unfair," perhaps here in this sentence you understand how you have proved my point.

The experience of talking with such a fool is captured perfectly by Bonhoeffer:

> "One feels...when talking to him, that one is dealing, not with the man himself, but with slogans, catchwords, and the like, which have taken hold of him. He is under a spell..."

And now, without knowing it, we have a massive contingent of this country under two different spells of folly: one is stuck in a hamster wheel of repeating Fox News jargon, another caught in a Woke Twitter maze of their own algorithmic making. Talking past one another, the two sides are no longer people, but avatars of their former selves repeating the uninteresting and predictable rhetoric of each ideological base. Bonhoeffer would call them, "passive instrument[s]...capable of any evil and at the same time incapable of seeing that it is evil."

This is the modern danger, the most insidious evil of our day. We are no longer liberated, responsible citizens, but shells of our personality, warped into profiles that give the appearance of ourselves without our very nature. Scrolling through our timelines, we numb ourselves out of our civic responsibilities and familial duties to engage with emotional rhetoric, scouring for what matches or offends our current temperament so we can either react with praise or disdain. Meanwhile, we do not know the names of our neighbors, we have little idea who our co-workers are, we're unclear on propositions we must vote for, unwilling to serve anyone or be inconvenienced by the needs of an acquaintance. In this kind of existence (and that's all that it is), there is little room for a consistent life of prayer or reflection, boredom and creativity. We continue to yell in all-caps at the blaze on the "other" side, not knowing we're stoking the fire.

The irony is this: the very anger we believe tears down the other side only emboldens it. This led to my confusion as to why everyone was so shocked by the first Presidential debate for the 2020 election. What did you expect? It was compared to bad theater by Stephen Colbert,[62] but I don't think it was theater at all — it was a mirror: looking at two old men shouting over each other with very little understanding of local responsibility (family, neighbor, county health, school systems), interrupting one another as they prepared their next remark that would be sparked by a key phrase or slogan from the other. All I saw was Twitter and Facebook materialized. I saw the vast wasteland of American dialogue in human form. I saw us. I saw folly.

* * *

And so how does one get out? Where is wisdom? Of course, Bonhoeffer's answer is ready and waiting: liberation and suffering. First, "a person's inward liberation to live a responsible life before God is the only real cure for folly." And finally, "We

---

[62] The clip is on YouTube: https://www.youtube.com/watch?v=tnN8OOtkwkM

have to learn that personal suffering is a more effective key, a more rewarding principle for exploring the world in thought and action than personal good fortune."

For Bonhoeffer, Christians are those who, with "Christ's large-heartedness," are liberated to lose. Perfectly free because of Christ's work, we are not bound to ideological victories. We are responsible to embrace our own defeat. We will lose the culture wars; the battle for "religious liberty" or "freedom," or "the truth" that we demand to be fought for us will be cast asunder. The cross is clear: there is no earthly triumph promised for the Christian; no politic, theory, constitution, or philosophy will be celebrated for us. The message of the cross is, itself, "the power and wisdom of God" (1 Corinthians 1:24), meaning it will be a "stumbling block" (literally in the Greek, *scandalon*: "a scandal") to those fixated on secular thinking.

When your own political ideologies, opinions about media, and critiques of culture are saving you, you will refuse to let them go, and thus, be a fool. The whole reason you find it difficult to *not* communicate your opinions, let alone change them, is because they function as a savior: without them, you are not you. If you change your mind, you change your identity. Do you see just how dangerous it is to host an immovable mind? And so beware: as you tightly hold on to the various "sources" that grant you a false peace of "being right," you will never see the wisdom of the cross—the wisdom that tells you to do precisely what you fear: lay it all down. So long as your beliefs assuage your fear and bolster your assurance about life, the cross will not. Hold tightly to your psyche and you will lose your mind (Matthew 16:25).

What separates a Christian from anyone else is not that they possess the truth, but that the truth possesses them: "the love

81

of Christ controls us," Paul says (2 Corinthians 5:14). And so it does. Being loved by Christ means we do not need to be right; we were *made right* in his death. This "being made right" is not in the ideological sense, but the theological sense—it is *righteousness*. Because we are right with God, we need not stress about having the right ideas. We can freely seek the truth without insisting to everyone everywhere that they *think* like us because our thinking never saved us in the first place. Our opinions can and will change, our minds are flexible, our posture is humble, because we don't hold on to such things for a kind of essential purpose. Our life is hidden with Christ in God (Colossians 3:3). We remain confidently here, in union with Christ, because of that doctrine, not because of an ideology. Why panic post on social media in hopes that your friends might "know the truth"? Why freak out when you see a dissenting opinion? Why reject an outside perspective? The cross stands as the great rebuke to a foolish, stubborn world set in their "opinions" as God himself took the most foolish thing (a cross) and created within it a well of wisdom:

> 27 But God chose what is foolish in the world to shame the wise; God chose what is weak in the world to shame the strong; 28 God chose what is low and despised in the world, even things that are not, to bring to nothing things that are, 29 so that no human being might boast in the presence of God.
>
> -1 Corinthians 1:27–29

A Christian does not know much for certain, except for this they can be sure: Jesus Christ died for sins and rose from the grave. This singular, certain, historic truth guides how we think about every idea that comes our way.

8

Ideological case study: racism

"Christianity has been almost sentimental in its effort to deal with hatred of human life...It has hesitated to analyze the basis of hatred and to evaluate it in terms of its possible significance in the lives of the people possessed by it."

-Howard Thurman, *Jesus and the Disinherited*

* * *

How does ideology operate and what might it look like? If it truly is a danger, and if Christianity is *not* an idea or set of ideas, then how does it operate in our life? And what happens when an idea or ideology comes so close to the core doctrines of faith? How can we think through that?

The next two chapters provide two case studies, as it were, of two prominent and dangerous ideologies: racism and nationalism. Why these two? First, because they have become points of division within the church in America. And secondly, I often hear and see Christian language appropriated onto both. My hope is that you will see how to think through an ideology in light of the person and work of Jesus. To use C.S. Lewis' metaphor of the sun from chapter 1, I'm pointing at some objects (ideas or ideologies) here while reminding you the only way to see it correctly is acknowledge that the sun has risen (the event of Christ's coming), thereby allowing you to see it in the first place.

Racism and white supremacy are ideologies—sets of ideas—that are abhorrent, wicked, and, as I will show now, demonic. These ideologies come from documents like *The Doctrine of Discovery* (1493),[63] where European elites used theological terms to deem black bodies inferior to white bodies, thus carving a path for a guilt-free genocide and slave trade. These authors could never have predicted what would come after these atrocities — they already displayed their stupidity just in the writing of the aforementioned document. But what came next was a cascade of ideas about black and brown people that led to the systemic oppression of millions of human beings, a reality we're still seeing the effects of right now: slavery, Jim Crow, redlining, mass incarceration, police brutality, and every other evil thing done to black people throughout this country's history (this is all without mentioning the further atrocities done to Indigenous people and other people of color).

A system of ideas (racism and white supremacy) led to systemic injustice; ideology bred iniquity. Could it be true

---

[63] The Upstander Project has a solid summary of this, which can be found online here: https://upstanderproject.org/learn/guides-and-resources/firs t-light/doctrine-of-discovery

that while they could have never predicted it, an outside force could have? While the original agitators of racism couldn't have organized it into such a lethal force, isn't it bizarre that it *has been* organized as such a lethal force?

Racism is *so* evil and *so* pervasive across so many countries and points in history, it warrants a thought that perhaps this did not come from the inside of the world of "flesh and blood" *only*, but outside also. Human beings are culpable for the evils of this world, but it must be at least considered that an "ideology" like white supremacy comes both "according to human tradition" and "to the elemental spirits of this world" (Colossians 2:8). As I have argued, both history *and* spiritual warfare play into any ideology, but racism in particular should be seen through the lens of the two previous categories.

Christians believe we do not only live in a world of human action and God's actions, but a world with human actions, God's actions, and the actions of his Enemy. There are, according to the New Testament, "the cosmic powers over this present darkness...the spiritual forces of evil" (Ephesians 3:10, 6:13). We are not alone in this world. We hear many voices and many of them are simply demonic.

* * *

The hesitation with this viewpoint is that it might relieve a racist from their responsibility. But it in fact does the opposite. Notice how the Scriptures view things: looking back at Colossians 2:8, we see it is not "the Devil's fault" alone for "taking captive" the minds of believers, but rather it is the believers. "See to it," Paul commands. He says, "*You* be sure that no one takes you captive by philosophy and empty deceit,

86

according to human tradition, according to the elemental spirits of the world, and not according to Christ" (Colossians 2:8). And here's Paul again in his intro to the Roman church:

> 21 For although they knew God, they did not honor him as God or give thanks to him, but they became futile in their thinking, and their foolish hearts were darkened. 22 Claiming to be wise, they became fools...
>
> -Romans 1:21–22

For emphasis, note: *"They* became futile in *their* thinking... *they* became fools."* While the darkness is mentioned in both passages, the onus is on the human beings. Just like in the Garden of Eden in Genesis 3, it's not *just* Satan who receives consequences after the forbidden fruit is eaten, but both Adam and Eve are culpable in their sin (Genesis 3:14–24). "Human tradition" and "the elemental spirits of this world" work together to create chaos and evil. The seed language of Genesis is helpful: Satan (demonic forces) plants and sows it, plans and prepares it; human beings give water and nurture it, bringing to fruition the very things that oppose God (human tradition). A biblical view of spiritual warfare need not select such strict categories of "demonic" *or* "human," but rather sees the world as including both categories with (sometimes) unclear or little distinction.[64]

Why is it important to insist on racism's inherent *spiritual*

---

[64] While Western people tend to shy away from talking about the demonic and spiritual reality, many non-Western cultures freely accept the spiritual world. For an excellent African perspective on this, see Esther E. Acolatse, *Powers, Principalities, and the Spirit: Biblical Realism in Africa and the West* (Eerdmans, 2018).

nature? Because it means we can say what it precisely is: from Satan, demonic, evil, perverse, anti-Christ. Using the strongest language possible, we do not say that racists have a "different viewpoint" than us or that they are "on the other side of the argument." We instead say what they are: captive to demonic thinking, imprisoned by satanic ideology.

* * *

By beginning to call racism and white supremacy demonic, we now can offer the solution of repentance for the Spirit of God to "renew the minds" (Romans 12:1–2) and the gospel message to prove it has "disarmed the rulers and authorities and put them to open shame" (Colossians 2:15). No, it does not mean that we "pray it away," with a kind of Pentecostalism that surreptitiously and simultaneously produces passion and sloth, nor does it mean we do not engage in the righteous work of political activity. Instead, I mean that we are able to present Christians with the truth of of their own book and Spirit, which leads to "all truth" (John 16:13). There is a way out.

Racism, again, is not a matter of opinion; it is an offense, and that offense has been defeated in the cross of Jesus Christ. Racism is not a new offense to the gospel, but one Paul battled in his day as did Jesus. Addressing the sinful ideology of racism to the Ephesian church (c. 65 AD), Paul declared the confrontational work of the cross against such hateful distinctions of black and white or, in his case, "Jew and Gentile":

> 13 But now in Christ Jesus you who once were far off have been brought near by the blood of Christ. 14 For

he himself is our peace, who has made us both one and has broken down in his flesh the dividing wall of hostility 15 by abolishing the law of commandments expressed in ordinances, that he might create in himself one new man in place of the two, so making peace, 16 and might reconcile us both to God in one body through the cross, thereby killing the hostility.

-Ephesians 2:13–16

Notice the "dividing wall of hostility" (understood and named today as "racism" or the "racist ideology") had to be "broken down," not rearranged, explained or debated. Alongside such destruction provided in the cross came the "abolishing" of religious laws and ordinances that were cultural and societal. Along with the destruction of the ideology came the destruction of the systems that kept the two ethnicities apart for so long. Now, Paul argues, there is "one new man in place of the two, so making peace." God, in Christ, has destroyed our foolish thinking, broken the bonds of demonic forces, one of which being the ideology of racism *and* the racist structures that come with such a Satanic philosophy.

So while the ideology of racism is, in fact, real and horrific, the Christian does not inherit this system of ideas in their new life hidden in Christ (Colossians 1:27, 3:4), but instead "what is earthly in you" must be "put to death" (Colossians 3:5). Racism (along with all ideological spells) is broken wherever the gospel is received. In Jesus Christ, there is a "new man in place of the two" (Ephesians 2:15), we then...

> "must put them all away: anger, wrath, malice, slander, and obscene talk from your mouth. 9 ...seeing that you have put off the old self with its practices 10 and have put on the new self, which is being renewed in knowledge after the image of its creator. 11 Here there is not Greek and Jew, circumcised and uncircumcised, barbarian, Scythian, slave, free; but Christ is all, and in all"
>
> -Colossians 3:7–11

From the start of the church, the "putting to death" of things in order to live life in Christ was prominent, especially with racism. Racism is not a uniquely American problem, nor a unique problem to the last few centuries. The demonic ideology of racism was there at the inception of the faith, which is why Paul wrote about it so clearly. Justin Martyr is one of the earliest Christian voices that we have after the writing of the New Testament. He lived between 100–165 AD and he wrote things that we have in publication to this day. In one of his writings he says,

> "We used to hate and destroy one another and refused to associate with people of another race... Now, because of Christ, we live together with such people and pray for our enemies."[65]

The answer to racism is nothing short of rebuke and repentance. We have no need for discussion about "different sides" of the

---

[65] Justin Martyr, *The First Apology.*

argument. The argument is over at the foot of the cross. Converting to Christianity will mean all our ideologies die, but the demonic ones need to go first. To, in any way, separate myself from the Black experience, Asian experience, etc., is to deny the very work of the cross. This work has created not a new group of various individuals all pursuing a kind of vague spiritual feeling, or an assortment of brains that can articulate similar truth statements, but one Church, one Body, of which I am just one "member." Together, we are not tied by ideological jargon, but by the Living Christ. This does not mean we abandon our culture and experiences—in fact the very opposite. We can now stand beneath the cross *with* our cultural experiences for the very reason that we know they do not threaten our identity as Christ's church, but rather illuminates it. Like a mosaic or a human body, it is precisely the distinctions and differences that make the whole thing beautiful and affecting.

The cross has re-created my life and placed it within the context of a multi-ethnic, global family. I, in fact, do not live anymore (Galatians 2:20). I am dead. Christ lives in me, and his operating effect in my daily experience is that I view the pain and suffering of others as my own, "bearing burdens" (Galatians 6:1–5) — and I do this more and more naturally as I understand that this is precisely what Christ has done for all, and lastly but fully, for me.

9

Ideological case study: nationalism

"A country is something that happens to you."
-Hanif Abdurraquib, *A Little Devil in America: Notes
in Praise of Black Performance*

* * *

B eing alive on January 6th was a strange experience. At the time, the COVID-19 pandemic was in its second, more deadly run. I was at home, working, when my friend texted me: "So, do we live in a totalitarian state NOW or what?" I replied with a simple question mark and he wrote back quickly, "Get on Twitter" (which is the new form of "turn on your TV). It wasn't long until I saw the chaos of the assault on the nation's capital that I *did*, in fact, turn on my television to see the carnage.

It was, as they say, in the Lord's timing that I saw the scene that has forever stuck in my memory: a cross erecting as the

Capitol was run over by idiot insurrectionists. Before I knew it, I had missed a mid-day Zoom meeting and was about to be late to pick up my son from his daycare. I was locked in to a scene that did not look like the country I grew up in, but also looked exactly like the country I grew up in. Here we saw the primitive nature of stupid people: running over the very structures they claim to celebrate and hold dear. The same people offended at mistreating a flag are now breaking windows of the Capitol Building. Once the irony settled in, the sadness came with it.

But that cross stuck with me. I knew, as a pastor, I'd have to think long and hard about what and how that kind of thing could happen. But I also needed to think about how to tell people that a cross being at that riot is the most obvious thing in the world. And I would also have to tell people that I would have been surprised if a cross *wasn't* at that riot, which would also raise all kinds of questions.

In America, nationalism and Christianity are so tied together, it's hard for many people to understand they are, in fact, different. The cross is "tangled up" in red, white, and blue, as Brian Zahnd has said.[66] And the sad truth about the scene at the Capitol that day is that all of those people were discipled to that point.

What do I mean when I say they were "discipled" to that place? I mean someone instructed them to that spot. Not many people wake up and decide to take a giant cross to an insurrection. There were small steps, little moments of instruction from people in positions of power and perceived intelligence and authority that slowly led each insurrectionist to that place. Each

---

[66] Zahnd has given this talk several times, I believe, and one version is available here on YouTube: https://www.youtube.com/watch?v=vBLXa9FEaI8

person who publicly claimed Christ at the insurrection was, at some point, given theological permission ("false teaching" in the New Testament) that malformed their moral imagination to that place.[67] Someone told them that Jesus would do what they did, and because they believed that lie, they showed up with a cross or a sign or a t-shirt that communicated so much.

There is a long, long history of such things and, at some level, the alarm that Christians had over Twitter made me wonder if they'd ever read about, oh I don't know, the history of the Christian faith? The cross has probably been used properly and improperly in an even split. The Christian message is daily taken to bizarre places in politics and culture, so no surprise should be noted here. What should be noted, however, is that we're certainly seeing a glaring example of such misuse.

Much of what we saw on January 6th involved a theological issue: someone believed something about Jesus Christ and moved to immoral action. January 6th was also a political, social, and psychological event, but we should not forget it was deeply theological. The New Testament is fraught with warnings against false teaching and false teachers. There is no way to read the entire canon of Scripture and believe that we

---

[67] The Biblical scholar Ellen Charry reminds us that the Pharisaic movement was quite popular (and gaining popularity) in Jesus' day because "they offered clarity, stability, and perhaps most significantly, a plan for securing the ritual purity that had been available in Jerusalem" (Ellen Charry, *By the Renewing of Your Minds: The Pastoral Function of Christian Doctrine* (Oxford University Press, 1999), pg. 63. Interacting with this, the Old Testament scholar Ellen Davis says that Matthew's gospel was a form of "prophetic discipleship," re-teaching and re-imagining a new path of life for those caught in such ideological garbage. See Ellen F. Davis, *Biblical Prophecy: Perspectives for Christian Theology, Discipleship, and Ministry* (Westminster John Knox Press, 2014), pgs. 210-217.

should be soft about such things.

And for as much as I could show various verses about false teaching, they rarely work to persuade. Instead, they seem to vilify when thrown at any issue we pick. I'd like to do something else. I'd like to offer a moment at the end of Jesus' life to show the ideology of nationalism versus the power of the kingdom of God. Again, the gospel is not an idea. Jesus, in this scene, is talking to Pilate, and they are not discussing ideas. Jesus is not in a battle of ideas. He is attempting cosmic, cruciform battle. He is fighting the powers of darkness. And he will tell you so much:

> 33 So Pilate entered his headquarters again and called Jesus and said to him, "Are you the King of the Jews?" 34 Jesus answered, "Do you say this of your own accord, or did others say it to you about me?" 35 Pilate answered, "Am I a Jew? Your own nation and the chief priests have delivered you over to me. What have you done?" 36 Jesus answered, "My kingdom is not of this world. If my kingdom were of this world, my servants would have been fighting, that I might not be delivered over to the Jews. But my kingdom is not from the world."
>
> -John 18:33-36

There is much for this pastor to note here, but I'll keep it to the ceremonial "three points and a conclusion."

1. Jesus' forms of rulership operate outside of, but adjacent to, political power.

Talking with Pilate, the primary political leader of the region, Jesus of Nazareth reveals his actual origins. Although he primarily exists within the landscape of Pilate's reality, he also exists entirely above it. He is "the Living and Abiding Word" (1 Peter 1:23), the *Logos* of God come as flesh (John 1:14). He came into this world and he will leave the world because he comes from another one, an entirely different plane of history. He is the only one who *came* to earth. The rest of us began here; he did not.

This is important to know when thinking through ideological captivity because every system of ideas that captures us is "of this world." But Jesus Christ is *not* of this world and says so directly in the above citation (John 18:36). Jesus has a kingdom and it is not made of the same materials as this system of existence.

This means that the Christian will find himself or herself consistently uncomfortable with any one set of ideas. Don't get me wrong, we Christians will have plenty of ideas. We will always consider The Beatles to be superior to the Stones (they are), or fiercely believe the 2-3 zone is the best for of defense in college basketball (it's not), or hold various staunch opinions about Robert F. Kennedy's assassination (it happened), or have all kinds of ideas about paper straws or the perfect dog leashes or the ideal ice cube—we will not be short on ideas and opinions! We will fight and discuss and laugh about all of those and more. But these ideas, while they make us into a kind of a person, they are not, in any way, consequential to our overall happiness. Christians, because they are saved and formed by the Eternal One, hold *all* ideas regarding politics, culture, art, etc. with a kind of open hand. Think quickly about the implications of enjoying art. Many Christians go crazy as they dissect lyrics or a novel to parse our "right doctrine." This is to miss the point of art entirely and why so much "Christian art" is awful. Art pushes us, messes with us. It does not exist to "teach" us. If we are not always looking around for ideological conformity we can actually read a book and enjoy it, instead of dissecting it to death. This is because what we think *about* something is not as important as what we *do* about something.

The other-worldly kingdom allows for us to live inside a society that spins about all kinds of ideas with remarkable peace. Why? Because it doesn't matter what I *think* about the US government as much as it matter how I live within it. With the Sermon on the Mount being our primary handbook for "other worldly kingdom life," we realize we can obey it and live inside those other-worldly ethics inside, well, any world. You can obey the other-worldly teachings of the Sermon on the Mount inside of a prison or a Porsche (although Jesus might argue one of those environments will be easier than the other). You can practice your citizenship to the kingdom of God anywhere. There is no place we would ever be unable to practice Jesus' commands. So long as we are banking on the world, we will constantly try to fix it to the ideal conditions for our obedience. The other-worldly kingdom argues the opposite: there are no ideal conditions for the other-worldly kingdom so long as you live it inside the world. Living in the kingdom of God will mean constant tension with the kingdom of Man. Which brings me to how this ends for Jesus and for us.

2. This "other-worldly" way is the way of the cross—that is, it is "cruciform" in nature.

The very nature of Jesus' kingdom being "other worldly" might make us believe that it is domineering, authoritarian, and demonstrative over the physical world we live in. But this is not the case. The kingdom of God is "cross-shaped," or as theologians have put it, "cruciform." To be cruciform is to be shaped like the cross. It is Philippians 2 kind of life, of having the mind of Christ, "who, though he was in the form of God, did not count equality with God a thing to be grasped, 7 but emptied himself, by taking the form of a servant, being born in the likeness of men. 8 And being found in human form, he humbled himself by becoming obedient to the point of death, even death on a cross" (Philippians 2:6-8).

For all of the misrepresentations of the cross in the world's ideology, none of it is accurate unless it takes on its shape. You can parade the cross around, show the cross, talk about the cross, but if your actions are not dying of yourself, removing your ego, deflating your life, and laying down your rights, you are not operating in the same kingdom as Jesus. He says so much in the above text with the conversation with Pilate: "if my kingdom were of this world, my servants would have been fighting." And guess what? They're not fighting—why? Because that is not cruciform, it is not self-denying, it is not martyrdom. You will know Jesus' other worldly kingdom by this: lives will be laid down for others.

January 6th may have had a Christian ideology, but it did not have a cross-shaped action. Put another way, you can have a Christian ideology that is not New Testament Christianity—"Christless Christianity," as Bonhoeffer would say.[68] During the insurrection, power was being taken, not given up. And you will know something is not of this world when it dies only to live all the more. But so long as a group of people are trying to grab power, you can safely assume that you are looking at an ideology very much "of this world." It'll die someday and never live again. But the cross will bear witness to something that can never die because it was, first and foremost, not existing only in this reality. Being "from heaven" or "eternal" is not to mean Jesus and his way "exists forever," it more so means that it cannot be defeated no matter what happens. Our lives, when free of ideological captivity, will be un-killable. We may die, but we will live. Like Jesus himself, killing us will only make us truly live. A cruciform life is not afraid of losing everything because we follow someone who lost everything only to gain it all.

Of all the differences between modern protest movements and the civil rights movement of the 1960s, I would suggest the cruciform nature of the work of Martin Luther King Jr. as primary. His ministry is perhaps most known for its passivity: being arrested for *sitting* on a bus, or *sitting* at a counter, or simply walking across a bridge. These forms of protest were, in their very nature, a kind of laying down. Notice in the work of Martin Luther King Jr. there was no fighting—why? Because he was operating out of another dimension, the Kingdom of God.

---

[68]   Dietrich Bonhoeffer, *The Cost of Discipleship* (Touchstone, 1995).

3. The cross bears witness to the truth, not the other way around.

At the center of Christian teaching is truth, but this "truth" is a disclosed kind of truth that announced himself at creation, spoke to Abraham in the starry night, called to Moses from the burning bush, and led the slaves out of Egypt. He is the Hidden One of Heaven, as Katherine Sonderegger has called him, the one who *chooses* to disclose himself.[69] "For since, in the wisdom of God, the world did not know God through wisdom," Paul writes, "it pleased God through the folly of what we preach [that is, the cross of Christ] to save those who believe" (1 Corinthians 1:21). The truth Christians believe cannot be summed up in a kind of systematic theology. Despite great efforts, theology begins and ends at the cross of Jesus Christ: we start at the cross and move backwards and forwards, knowing that in Jesus crucified we see "the power of God and the wisdom of God" (1 Corinthians 1:24).

This is why much of Christianity looks foolish. This is why it seems backwards. It doesn't make sense to be killed for your faith, nor is it "wise" to be arrested while sitting at a counter. Preaching, especially today, seems ridiculous. Giving away our money and refusing the world's goods and praying will all seem quite absurd as we bring about our own apocalypse. But what else are we to do but die? As Christ-followers, we see the cross as the perfect revelation of who God is and where God stands: he is not revealed through the gaining of political power or the accumulation of proper resources for executing a

---

[69] Katherine Sonderegger, *Systematic Theology: Volume 1* (Fortress Press, 2015). This book is indispensable and a gift to theologians everywhere.

strategic mission. He is not primarily available to those with stock options and a diversified investment portfolio. God is on the cross. He is the lowly one, the dying criminal, the poor man on a tree, cursed for us. As we stare at the cross we see, then, the dramatic difference between the nature of God and the nature of man. God, unlike man, can be found in giving up. At the end of ourselves we find the beginning of God. But so long as we puff ourselves up and work together to grab governmental power, we will never find the kingdom of God.

"What is truth?"

Pilate's haunting question is our question at the end of this brief narrative in John's gospel: what *is* truth, exactly? The question hangs over the story and the scene switches after this. Jesus does not answer. Why? Why no answer to a perfectly good question from an extremely powerful person? Didn't Jesus miss an opportunity to evangelize and bring another dear child into the kingdom of heaven?

The answer to Pilate's question is not found in a sentence of John's gospel, but in every sentence of John's gospel put together. The entire thing is a witness to the reality of Jesus Christ as the way, the truth, and the life (John 14:6). The author says this much in the first chapter: "And the Word became flesh and dwelt among us, and we have seen his glory, glory as of the only Son from the Father, full of grace and truth" (John 1:14). Pilate's question was answered if only he had the eyes to see. Truth was sitting right before him. Better than the question, "What is truth?" Is the question, "Who is truth?" Truth is not found in sentimental, pithy statements or philosophical platitudes, it is found inside the very being of Jesus Christ, the Word.

This is important when talking about nationalism and the events of January 6ᵗʰ because it brings us to our very haunting conclusion: if everything done at the Capitol that day looked nothing like Jesus, revealed nothing of the cross, and instead showed us the opposite, then what were we looking at? What did we actually see on display?

I began this chapter by affirming that everyone at that rally was discipled to that place, and many of them were discipled to that place by a pastor—they were given theological permission to partake in an insurrection or watch it happen without any critique. Someone told them violence is compatible with a cross-shaped life. Someone lied to them and they believed it. Someone showed them a non-truth, selling it as truth itself.

But if truth is the person of Jesus, then what is the non-truth they were following? Well, I supposed I do not know for sure, but I can tell you one thing: all those who were praying at the riot, all those who held signs and erected crosses and sang worship songs were all, in my mind, singing and praying to someone who is not Jesus Christ. Yes, worship was happening, and yes, I know, people were praying, but worshiping what? And praying to who? If you worship Christ crucified, I'm afraid you would never find yourself enacting this kind of violence—or maybe any violence at all. If you embrace "the foolishness of the cross" (1 Corinthians 1:18), you would not panic if you lost political power. You would do something foolish to the world: you would prepare to die, knowing you would live.

There are, then, two ways to think about what happened on January 6th: an issue of discipleship and/or an issue of worship. Some gather around ideologies because they are taught the wrong thing by the wrong person (discipleship).

But others adopt ideologies because of spiritual forces that manipulate their minds (worship). The consistent warnings of the New Testament include fierce words about who we are following and what we are entertaining spiritually. Christians who are growing in wisdom and humility discern both the teachings they receive and the spirits they may be encountering. Remember, all of us can be fools, and it can happen in all kinds of ways.

10

Fools for Christ

"Fools for Christ have the gift, and the audacity, to manifest openly the human fall and sin which is common to us all: this is the reality of our nature, and it is not canceled out by individual cases of 'improvement,' not by concealment behind social externals."

-Christos Yannaras, *The Freedom of Morality*

* * *

I started this book by telling you many have become fools and that might be more dangerous than many people becoming evil. That thread has been woven throughout this book at different times and in different ways. These final three chapters will be brief, but will, hopefully, set a course towards wisdom and away from ideological captivity. We will need some encouragement to stand fast in what Bob Dylan has called the "idiot wind." And the only way, in my mind, to live wisely in Christ is to act a fool according to the world.

Christians have long been "fools for Christ," a phrase borrowed from St. Paul's letter to the Corinthians:

> 9 For I think that God has exhibited us apostles as last of all, like men sentenced to death, because we have become a spectacle to the world, to angels, and to men. 10 We are fools for Christ's sake, but you are wise in Christ. We are weak, but you are strong. You are held in honor, but we in disrepute. 11 To the present hour we hunger and thirst, we are poorly dressed and buffeted and homeless, 12 and we labor, working with our own hands. When reviled, we bless; when persecuted, we endure; 13 when slandered, we entreat. We have become, and are still, like the scum of the world, the refuse of all things.
>
> -1 Corinthians 4:9-13

The wisdom of the cross (and the cruciform life inside those who follow its path) will look insane to a person who has never encountered it. So for those imprisoned in ideological captivity, one who possesses slow, careful, and sacrificial wisdom will look bizarre. To an onlooker, the cross is weird. But it is certainly a compliment to be called an idiot by an idiot, right?

Church history has a funny relationship with being a fool for Christ. The most recent display in the late 90s was about being a "Jesus Freak," as DC Talk told us to be. "I don't really care if they label me a Jesus Freak / there ain't no disguising the truth."[70] But long before that, fathers and mothers of the church "played the fool" for Christ in order to illuminate the madness of the world. One way to show that the world has gone mad it to mirror their insanity back to them. And it's something Christians have long done.

* * *

In his book, *The Freedom of Morality*, Greek Orthodox theologian Christos Yannaras tells the story of those who "perform strange and senseless actions—the actions of a madman. Yet these actions always have a deeper meaning: they always aim to uncover the reality and truth hidden behind the practices of this world."[71] These men and women would get drunk in taverns, hang with prostitutes and gamblers, they'd live homeless or extravagantly rich. They would do this to show off the absolute absurdity of a Christian living in that way. They would often come out during major moments of the church's secularization—its melding with the world's morals and ways—in order to wake the church up from living just like everyone else. It's a hell of a strategy that I'd love to see happen today. The fools "sought the contempt of men, the utter degradation of their own ego, in order to gain that ineffable freedom and taste of life which comes as a gift when the last resistance of egocentric individuality is dead."[72] St. Andrew of Constantinople or St. Symeon of Emesa would do ridiculous things to get the attention of believers in hopes they would

---

[70] DC Talk, "Jesus Freak" (ForeFront/Virgin, 1995).

[71] Christos Yannaras, *The Freedom of Morality*, pg. 65

[72] Yannaras, *The Freedom of Morality*, pg. 69-70

finally see how low the church had sunk to the world's standards. Again, quite the evangelistic strategy.

But it is something for the church today to think about: how have we become so much like the world that we cannot see our own foolishness? Certainly the church in America could use some fools for Christ to show us just how consumerist and capitalistic we have become in our expression of the way of Jesus. Our churches are brands, our pastor's are leadership experts, and our programs are consumer products. We are all rated on Yelp, whether we like it or not, and we are all a few one star reviews away from some sort of demise.

Yes, some of this is just "the way things are," and yes, these things provide routes to discipleship and new life in Jesus Christ, but also much of it is unnecessary for the church's existence and development. What *must* we possess to be the church? Very little. It might mean that the church acts like fools in order to show the world its own folly. Paul said this much to the Corinthians, earlier in the letter:

> "27 But God chose what is foolish in the world to shame the wise; God chose what is weak in the world to shame the strong; 28 God chose what is low and despised in the world, even things that are not, to bring to nothing things that are, 29 so that no human being might boast in the presence of God."
>
> -1 Corinthians 1:27-29

And it's not like God just did this one time. It's not as if God simply chose Jesus Christ as the *one time* he would shame the wise through foolishness. No, remember that the cross bears witness to the truth, not the other way around. This is the way God *always* acts. God shames the wise with fools. And if we are going to live in a world of those who "claiming to be wise" but our idiots (Romans 1:22), we might need to look briefly at God's "foolish" ways:

Abraham, the man worshiping foreign gods and lying his way out of his home country, is used by God to begin the family of God (Joshua 24:2).

Sarah, his wife, bears a son at a ridiculous age after being barren for years (Genesis 21:1-2).

Jacob, the master manipulator and smooth-talker, betrays his own brother by lying to his father. He is nonetheless used to continue to story of Israel, God's people (Genesis 25:29-34).

God speaks in a burning bush to a murderer who is a horrible public speaker. This is Moses, perhaps the most important figure in Israel's history (Exodus 3:1-22).

Israel, in general, is a small nation of nobodies with no land or financial assets, they were lacking any political power or governmental structure. And then God decides to use them throughout human history as the profound witness to his name (Deuteronomy 9:1-12).

Rahab and Ruth and Tamar are all noted in the genealogy of Jesus. They are foreign women—non-Israelites—who have very little power and prestige but are used to show the wisdom of God (Matthew 1:1-17).

This is all not to mention all the prophets, who all acted like fools and who were all too young and unknown for God to really use them, but he did, providing his powerful presence through their spoken and written word: Esther, Isaiah, Jeremiah. God used a whale and a disobedient young prophet to save the nation of Nineveh.

And yes God chose a young girl, a teenage refugee to be the vessel for him to come to this planet as the word made flesh: Mary, the mother of God.

God uses the foolishness of the world to shame the strong. And so this makes me wonder: how do we, as God's people today, act a fool?

Consider how foolish the spiritual disciplines look today. Aside from fasting, none of them are hip. Prayer will always be something at which a workaholic culture will balk. Silence is profoundly stupid to a culture of blathering social media profiles. Solitude communicates unpopularity. Asceticism (the rejection of material goods) makes no sense and will harm our economy. Sabbath-keeping means you won't produce anything of value and will therefore not be useful to your company or this world. Forgiving someone who has damaged and hurt you does not feel great. Worshiping Jesus on Sunday seems useless to this world—why go to church when you can go to the beach or go on a hike and "feel" spiritual? The most freeing thing in the world is to obey Jesus Christ. You become liberated from humanity's constantly shifting rules when you abide by eternal ones.

* * *

The book of Hebrews includes a famous list of faithful fools for God. Some of the names I mentioned earlier can be found through most of Hebrews 11. After cataloging the obedient ones, the writer of this book starts to run out of gas: "Time would fail me," he writes, to tell about every person who walked the way of the cross with a kind of faithfulness that looked like foolishness to the world (Hebrews 11:32). He says there were people who "through faith...conquered kingdoms, enforced justice, obtained promises, stopped the mouths of lions," and most of them were "destitute, persecuted, and mistreated" (Hebrews 11:33, 37). They lived a life the world could not comprehend because it is a kind of life that transcends the very materials we exist inside. They lived eternal lives, which is confusing to those living temporal ones.

The writer closes the chapter by saying "the world was not worthy of them" (Hebrews 11:38). The world mistreats the citizens of the kingdom of God not because they are worse than the world, but because they are better. The world promises a false meritocracy: do good and good will be done to you. The gospel gives us life abundant: give your life away for the sake of God and others and you will have eternal life. This means that anyone can have life and life to the full. To live this kind of life will be to display a kind of beauty that is far too stunning for the world. I often think about this line when I encounter parents who serve their special needs children with grace and patience, or when I see caretakers of those with disabilities. Those who do this kind of work with generosity and humility are just too good for the world. We're not worthy of them. They are displaying a kind of behavior only fit for heaven.

Because the way of the cross is far better than the ways of the world, the only thing the world knows how to do is scoff. To most who do not know God, faithfulness looks like a waste of time. We all dismiss what we do not understand. And so such is the case for those who walk in the path of the cross. After all, our Lord and Master had this path. If we follow him, logic would say our life might look like his: "He was in the world, and the world was made through him, yet the world did not know him. He came to his own, and his own people did not receive him" (John 1:10-11).

May Christians be the ones who faithfully serve in low places, who give without reward, who parent without praise and who lead by sacrificing the earthly rewards. May we be the ones in secret, obscure places, doing a kind of work that cannot be captured on social media—and if it were, it would be boring. Could we be a witness that could only be seen by those looking for new life? There are so many ways to be a fool for Jesus. These practices—and so much more—might be the only way to stand fast in the winds of idiocy.

11

How to avoid ideological captivity

"The aim of our charge is love that issues from a pure heart and a good conscience and a sincere faith. Certain persons, by swerving from these, have wandered away into vain discussion, desiring to be teachers of the law, without understanding either what they are saying or the things about which they make confident assertions."

-1 Timothy 1:5-7

* * *

As a brief aside in an otherwise pedestrian virtual conference panel discussing the recent protests and national election, I heard John Mark Comer lament something I had not fully considered.[73] When asked about the most difficult aspect of ministry right now, Comer said he was grieving over just how many people he's known who have fallen captive to different ideologies—even people he has known for decades.

Suddenly, my mind awoke to a very similar notion — a lament in my own right — of all those who *I* have known who have slid down a cliff into some pre-packaged set of catch-phrases and simplistic beliefs curated for them by algorithms or cable television (or both) and all presented by uneducated performers who parrot some of the more predictable and uninteresting (not to mention, factually incorrect) ideas about reality. Then I got sad, too.

I'm sorry to report that I have no way of knowing if the previously described person is you. I pray it's not, but simple math would tell me that some of you reading this have tumbled down the ravine into "ideological captivity" (and yes, I am fully aware of this mixed metaphor and am loving it). What do we mean by this?

The prison of belief ("ideological captivity") exists in between the poles of QAnon adherents all the way to violent Antifa conspirators, but also exists on the dangerous spectrum in between such radical beliefs, not just the end points. Don't get me wrong, the extremes are real, but more insidious than radical thinking is the step before it: where we repost videos or articles that match our emotional temperament without fact-checking, or where we demand our followers to "do their research" (an absolutely asinine request of something they cannot do and

---

[73] He said this at an event hosted by Q in 2020, which can be found for purchase here: https://qanda.squarespace.com/

you, as you post, have actually not fully done), or the lazy regurgitation of rhetoric from accounts we follow with no nuanced comment from us, no hesitation about what we may be ingesting, no context. We blame tech companies for censoring too much or not censoring enough, failing to admit that "Big Tech" is not the internet's worst enemy—we are.

* * *

What pains me the most as a pastor is to see people chained to a kind of thinking they never developed themselves, but one that was sold through the algorithms created by consumer choices. It was offered and bought: "accounts you should follow" and retweets and "this person liked this post" all leads us towards a captivity of our own making. This is alive and well on the left through Woke Twitter, Aggregated Internet Explainers, and Instagram Justice Slides just as much as it blooms on the right through Media Skeptics, Untrained and Self-Proclaimed Journalists, and Faux Experts of medicine, theology, and politics. It's all bait, of course, and incredibly dangerous, but it's also humorless and stupid. If you find yourself offended at my examples, I'm afraid you're proving my point: if you cannot converse over your opinions, if you're unable to spar lightly and then listen to various forms of thinking, and if even considering another side of things feels like an attack, I'm afraid you do not have "beliefs," but idols.

This is what makes the whole thing a spiritual concern, a pastoral emergency: ideologies and idols have a cozy relationship. These verses have been on my mind for two years:

8 See to it that no one takes you captive by philosophy and empty deceit, according to human tradition, according to the elemental spirits of the world, and not according to Christ.

- Colossians 2:8

6 Let no one deceive you with empty words, for because of these things the wrath of God comes upon the sons of disobedience. 7 Therefore do not become partners with them...

- Ephesians 5:6–7

20 O Timothy, guard the deposit entrusted to you. Avoid the irreverent babble and contradictions of what is falsely called "knowledge," 21 for by professing it some have swerved from the faith.

- 1 Timothy 6:20–21

I could go on. But let me suggest that if Scripture so repeatedly warns us of ideological captivity, what makes us think we're immune to it? Perhaps before the aforementioned "slide" into such a prison of belief (still *loving* the mixed metaphor), there is an arrogance, a pride you might say, wherein we cannot fathom such a thing could even happen to us. But immaturity is just as possible as maturity; a dwarfed faith can happen just as easily as a growing one. You and I are not guaranteed a sound mind and are perfectly capable of spiritual deceleration through foolishness.

Do you believe you can be deceived? Are you, as Jesus

famously said, "wise as serpents?" Are you shrewd? Upon entering the hellscape that is the internet, do you find yourself skeptical of the articles that come up to the surface, or are you clicking with wild abandon as you wait for the next hit of the adrenaline that comes with a "discovery?" I have three thoughts for how we can avoid ideological captivity:

1. Reinstall the expert

This could be a whole book — well, it already is.[74] We have abandoned those who have trained for decades and somehow an educated person is suspicious. Instead, we want a presenter of information who matches our disposition. Now, the person who was thrown out of a university or training center for propping up asinine science or inconsistent professional work is now recast as the "maverick" who "the system" wanted to get rid of, not understanding that the role of a community of experts is to do precisely that: guard the public from insane ideas. We trust those who present information that matches our emotional temperament instead of those who have spent years germinating their ideas with humility. I know it's crazy, but there are people — many, many people — who know more than you and me, and our role is not to critique them, but listen to them and do what they tell us to do. I know you have a Twitter account and a phone, but they have a lifetime of study, discipline, and hard work that should humble you to the point of at least a bent ear.

Of course we must be discerning in who we follow, and of

---

[74] See Thomas Nichols, *The Death of Expertise: The Campaign against Established Knowledge and Why it Matters* (Oxford University Press, 2017).

course not all people with Ph.Ds are trustworthy, and no not everyone who has written a book or two or twenty is worth any of your time. And yes, of course, this is one thing that makes living in the 21st century so impossible. But it is also an opportunity to exercise your brain and think critically: who is this source you're reading and where are they coming from? Do other people in their field admire them? Who do they quote and who might quote them? Who endorses their work? What does your pastor think? What do other smart people in your life who think differently than you think about them? These might be good places to begin when understanding if you're listening to an expert or an impostor.

2. Read a freaking book

Every piece of information you hear seems "amazing" when you're not reading. You'll see a video, a Twitter thread, one of those Instagram posts with six slides of text...and you'll be thunderstruck. *Wow,* you think, *I never thought of it this way!* But maybe you never thought of it that way because you never thought about it in the first place. Every idea is incredible when you have no backdrop of wisdom, no lengthened argument you've been considering, no narrative rolling through your head that you have had to follow for over three hundred pages. Books extend the line of reasoning and require patience; they de-center your personal experience and force you to follow one thought or many thoughts over a longer span. Fiction or non-fiction, Scripture or a good hardcover, history, biography, science writing — all of it develops your mind to be less impressed with the short-form, intellectually inferior internet posts created to grab your attention and inflate someone's ego while they simultaneously deflate your brain. Books do not simply deliver information, they subversively teach you how to take it it too.

One concern we should label an emergency is the lack of literacy in today's Western culture. It's not that people cannot read, it's that they cannot read *well*. How many times have you heard an author interviewed about a book they wrote and convince yourself you "got the gist of it?" Or, after skimming an article, you talk confidently about the subject to your friends over drinks on a Thursday night? I am not convinced many people today notate books, make notes to themselves, or even discuss books in groups anymore. All of these practices (and so much more) develop true literacy. If we are going to avoid ideological captivity, we are going to need to read well.

3. Research inside a wide community

One common and ridiculous claim today is of the self-professed "researcher." This person (according to them and them only) has "done all the research" and comes back to us inferiors with the final answer to any given subject—anything from guns to autism. What they mean, generously, is that they have spent a *lot* of time on the internet and probably read one, maybe two books of one, maybe two perspectives. This, my friends, is not research. Research is a community based effort in the context of a peer reviewed process. It involves a community of authoritative, fact-checking criticism that is necessary for developing new ideas. In order to avoid the landslide of terrible ideas, consider aligning with (and following those who align with) credible institutions that set their ideas and research against a high level of accountability.

Even as a pastor, I submit to a) a lead pastor and b) an executive board, both of whom are responsible for guarding anything I teach. In addition to this, we pastors have gone through the crucible of seminary, wherein we dedicated our life for a number of years to study Scripture in a community of experts and peers who reviewed our work and gave us feedback on the things we were saying. Developing our ideas in community does not necessarily mean we are all to become academics, but it does mean we will model our "research" efforts off of this credible processes of accountability. If we do not do this, we must not claim to be experts, nor should we follow self-professed "experts" who have not committed themselves to such a process. We will also be disinterested in performers and presenters, who, for one reason or another, have podcasted/videoed their way to a large platform without answering to anyone who actually knows something about the subject.

4. Go to church

Sundays are where you step outside of yourself and into the story of Jesus Christ. We sing to get outside of us and set our minds on that which is worthy of adoration. We listen instead of speaking. We eat bread and drink wine with people unlike us. We stare into something mysterious and remember the death of Christ. We sit and then stand and then sit again. We say hi to people whose names we forget. All of these actions have the ability to do something profound to any human being: humble us. To engage in a weekly activity that fosters humility will help us in our pursuit of freedom. It does not guarantee it, but a good church will help.[75]

It could be us

As you may well know, there are many more paths to prison, both actual and ideological. Sliding into the confines of a belief system can happen in many other ways, but why write another 2,000 words? There is the over-emphasis on *one* teacher, the embrace of binary thinking, an underdeveloped sense of reason, etc., etc...all this and more is dangerous. I will end with this: *no one is safe from ideological captivity.* I do not write this as one who has claimed to escape, but rather as one who has the potential of cascading towards a kind of foolishness at which I currently balk. The aforementioned Scriptural warnings are not given to *some* Christians, but all Christians — all people for that matter! Perhaps in thinking that we are incapable of becoming ideological fanatics, we have already begun the slide downward. To stay humble will mean to stay vigilant with our minds, second-guessing the information given to us, and committing ourselves to a trusted community where ideas can flourish and, if need be, die the death they deserve.

---

[75] May I emphasize "good" in the phrase "good church" here? Because another pastoral grief of mine has been the rise of so many churches—whole groups of people—who are stuck in ideological captivity. It is most certainly the fault of the leadership and the Lead Pastor in nearly all of these circumstances, but please, let's all empty these churches that claim the name of Jesus but sell a set of ideas that sound exactly like the internet. Look for leaders who are humble, biblically literate, careful, kind, generous, and courageous.

12

Rules for staying sane

"Dearly beloved
   We are gathered here today
   To get through this thing called life…"
                                        -Prince, "Let's Go Crazy"

* * *

There are so many ways to stay sane. This is far from a complete list. As you might guess, I am completely unqualified to write any of this (but since when did that stop me?) as I have mostly disobeyed these commands for many years. Nevertheless, in reviewing this book, I sensed the need for something annoyingly "practical" (a word I despise but recognize as important). While I tried to stay away from the obvious, I could not do so entirely, and so, well, here it is: my list of rules to stick to in order to not go completely crazy and end up in an ideological prison of your own making.

1. Consider the lilies

Jesus Christ instructed us, that when we sense a creeping anxiety about life's provisions, we should "consider the lilies of the field, how they grow: they neither toil nor spin" (Matthew 6:27). It is interesting that the Greek here, *katamathe*, is only used here in the New Testament, and speaks to a deep consideration for ultimate understanding. This is about looking very closely and intently at something to seek some form of knowledge you did not previously possess.

In a world of screens, 15 second Instagram stories, and pithy tweets, it takes a level of discipline to stare at a flower. And yet, notice what happens to your brain when you stare at something God has made: things slow down. This goes beyond "stop and smell the roses," and turns into a kind of reflection that will help you calm the spinning reality of the internet.

2. Spend time with children

Children are the most free beings on the planet. They have no reservations about their personality and they are incredibly presumptuous. No small child second guesses themselves. It's very, very freeing. You may have children, you may not, but how can you surround yourself with some? Could you volunteer in the children's ministry at church? Or watch your friends' kids for free so they could go on a date? Perhaps you could make an effort to be with more tiny people who walk around the world freely. Watching my two-year-old son walk around, I can see in his eyes a single thought: that everything he is currently doing he believes to be the exact right thing to do. He is that free. I am not. I constantly second guess my actions and exist in a kind of self-consciousness that is difficult to escape. Jesus told us that "unless you turn and become like children, you will never enter the kingdom of heaven" (Matthew 18:3). How will we become like children if we never spend time with them? Our world is crazy mostly because people have tricked themselves into thinking they are rational, exceptional creatures. We are finding out they most certainly are not.

3. Puzzles or the guitar: you choose

"A slack hand causes poverty," says Proverbs 10:4. Of course the context of this verse has to do with manual labor (work), but you're not a farmer are you (or are you)? Nevertheless, kinesthetic activity is better than mindlessly doomscrolling. Concentrating your brain and hands on a complex physical/mental activity like a puzzle or an instrument will help your brain take a break from the constant assault of information that comes from your phone. You'll also realize how difficult puzzles actually are and the frustration will be good for you. Puzzles are the golf of cabin activities: you play yourself and you usually lose...which only makes you want to get back out there and try again.

4. Pray

Talk to God and listen to God and converse with God as much as possible. Pray your own prayers or prayer the prayers of others. Pray the Psalms. Pray the Lord's Prayer. Pray from *The Book of Common Prayer* or *The Valley of Vision*. Did you really think I'd make it through this list without telling you that prayer is perhaps the most sane thing you can do when the world is going mad? Either God will change the craziness or will change the way you receive it. Both would be beneficial, so maybe put this book down for a second and say a prayer.

5. Engage with satire as much as the news

For every chunk of 20 minutes you spend scrolling a news app or taking it in however you take it in, engage with someone satirizing it. I do not mean someone making fun of the news or cracking jokes about the news: late night talk shows like John Oliver or Trevor Noah have their place, but that is not satire. Those are jokes. Jokes are great but it is satire that makes you think even more. Satire is the use of humorous narrative to expose the sins of the world, particularly the political ones. It is the ability to form a construction of humor that slices through painful contemporary issues. This is Dave Chappelle, *South Park*, and the novels of Sam Lipsyte or Christopher Buckley. Satire is found in sketch comedy or theater or even music. Listening or watching or reading these voices is not just to laugh at the things you do not believe, but the things you do. Satire gives us the gift of laughing at beliefs we may hold so tightly we do not realize we're becoming arrogant. If you are unable to laugh at your opinions you are, without question, a major bummer.

6. Listen to an entire album

I love (and make) a good playlist, but your brain requires a different level of attention when you listen to a whole album. Not only are you able to see if the artist is actually any good at constructing a larger project and not just "a good song," but you are able to tell something about your own attention span for art. I do not mean you need to sit in front of your Sonos speaker or Bluetooth device and listen to 45 minutes of the new War on Drugs album (although you should), but perhaps let the album run through the first hour of your road trip—the whole album. Or put it on when you clean your house. As an amateur vinyl collector, I've realized the difference it has made in my understanding of the world to not just listen to "Isn't She Lovely?" but to instead listen to the entirety of *Songs in the Key of Life*. Something changes.

7. Go to an art museum and let it mess with you.

Sculptures and paintings and installations and photographs evoke something in our brain that is healthy and that is really lacking in our current culture. We like looking at cool designs online, but it has regressed our understanding of art. It has led to the blasé aesthetic of the modern world: everything is macrame and neutral, poorly imitating Chip and Joanna Gaines with tight, tan leather couches next to old pipes that have been repurposed as light fixtures. This is not art. This does not provoke anything in you or disturb you. This kind of thing calms you down and fills you with envy and greed, which is why it is so celebrated in America. Art messes with you, confuses you even, and can (at its best) open you up to a new form of consideration about reality. Just go to the nearest museum of modern art, or a university's exhibit. Just go.

8. Sweat

Here's one I definitely do not do enough but one by which my wife lives. Exercising changes your physiology. I don't have much more to say about it because I am, as they say, an "indoorsman," but I would be healthier and more sane if my heart rate increased with more regularity in the context of physical exercise. You would too.

9. Stare out a window

When was the last time you did this? Try it for an absurd amount of time.

10. Hang out with old people and ask them questions

I purposefully did not write "older" people because it is not enough for people to just "have a few years on you." No, you need to spend time with geezers, the elderly, the sages. People who have like 30 years on you. And you need to come ready to ask them questions that are interesting. I recently asked my 88 year-old grandmother what she thinks the major differences are with raising children now verses when she was raising her kids in the 50s and 60s. Her first thought was that she used to wrap my uncle up when he was an infant and shove his head in the corner of the backseat of the car because "there were not any car seats." She assured me he was safe because "his four year old brother kept a hand on him." What a lovely conversation. In between these hilarious moments, people much older than you will offer you profound wisdom with a kind of obviousness that is shocking. That same grandmother of mine that laid a baby of hers on the back bench of a Buick has given me some of the greatest insights about church, family, and life.

11. Read poetry and fiction

Keeping your mind on a longer or more artistic form of reading helps you see how stupid internet language is. Everything will be mind blowing to you on the internet if you're not reading. You'll think some video is amazing or some tweet is hilarious or some post is insightful, but this is because your baseline for interest has been depleted to the sophomoric style of those online. Reading poetry (good poetry, might I add) or a novel will help your brain sustain a longer narrative or argument, or help you see the possibility words and stories have, which far exceed the possibilities of the things you hear on a podcast or read in a Buzzfeed article.

Live an embodied life

Looking through this list, it should be noted that most (if not all) of the examples I am giving here as a way out of ideological captivity are *embodied* practices: they are all things we do that allow us to recognize our finite nature.[76] Embodiment gives us a sacramental vision of the world. A "sacramental" vision affirms we do not live in a cosmos divorced from God's presence in any way. Rather, we live in a universe where God has left his divine imprint on every living thing he has created. With

---

[76] I owe this insight to Calum Hayes and Naseem Khalili, who both gave me this note separately as they read early drafts.

a sacramental or embodied mindset, we meet God inside the finite nature of our existence, not apart from it. The practices mentioned above are embodied practices wherein our mind is renewed to the sacramental nature of reality: God is here and near.

We are more prone to ideological captivity when we live a *disembodied* faith.[77] A disembodied faith would mean that we nourish our souls through online sermons, digital communities, social media content, and inspirational videos. This kind of faith lives in our heads and not in our bodies. We never *go* to church or eat a meal with Christian friends or raise our hands in worship. So long as we disembody our faith, communion will never mean much, singing will just be a precursor to the sermon, and "community" will be theory instead of showing up to your friend's house with your Bible on a Tuesday night. The material world is not a place for Christians to ignore, rather it is the very environment in which we are told to rest and receive God. You cannot love God in theory.

Perhaps the final word for us, a benediction of sorts, is to remember that the spiritual disciplines are given to us to center our lives in Christ, to allow the love of God to be the gravity by which we walk: to pray, read Scripture, worship and sing with other Christians, to fast, be still and silent, to take communion together, to pray in the presence of enemies and friends, and practice a regular Sabbath...all of this is for us. They all invite us to an embodied faith. So long as we do not engage in the disciplines, we will stumble out of humility and wisdom and

---

[77] For a better and longer treatment of this, see my friend Jay Y. Kim's work: *Analog Church: Why We Need Real People, Places, and Things in the Digital Age* (IVP, 2020) and *Analog Christian: Cultivating Contentment, Resilience, and Wisdom in the Digital Age* (IVP, 2022).

into our self-righteous brain. Would God expect us to be sane and humble if we reject his clearly commanded teachings? How can we expect to be great in faith if we lack the very disciplines to build it? In such chaotic times, a subversive spirituality is needed. Let's give Dallas Willard the last word:

> "Who are the great ones in The Way, what are the significant movements in the history of the church that do *not* bear the deep and pervasive imprint of the disciplines for spiritual life? If there are none, what leads us to believe that *we* might be an exception to the rule...?"[78]

---

[78] Dallas Willard, *The Spirit of the Disciplines* (HarperOne, 1999), pg. 126.

A prayer for wisdom

God and Father of all wisdom,

Grant me the ability to discern what is good, pleasing, beneficial, and necessary.

Guard me from the temptations of easy-believing, from the snare of foolishness that I know I am not above. Help me, O God, as I live in a world inundated with information but empty of wisdom.

Forgive me, in Christ's name, for being too quick, too confident, and too fearful. Release me from any bonds of bad thinking that I am in right now. I need your Holy Spirit to guide me as I think. Grant me the strength of heart and mind to think critically, but not cynically, to gain true wisdom.

Lead me to speak when I am wanting to be silent, to be silent when I am wanting to speak, and for the wisdom to know the difference between these things.

As I receive all of this from you, Father, and continue to think, life, and act in step with your Holy Spirit, please keep me humble, gracious, patient, and kind, as your Son Jesus displayed with perfection. I pray this in his name.

Amen.

Acknowledgments

All authors complete books in massive debt to countless people. I am no exception. The loving, steady, and gracious presence of my wife, Ali, remains the most important part of any book I've written. She lives with my weird brain and is one of the best readers I know, and her early thoughts on anything I write is essential to everything I produce. I also want to thank our son, Jude, who is not yet three years-old, but who inspires us every day to remember how futile book writing really is and how living together under God's grace is our primary satisfaction here and for eternity. He's the best.

I'd like to thank Matthew Wimer, George Callihan, and everyone at Wipf & Stock Publishers for their early and enthusiastic support of this book. Thank you for your generosity and also for giving me a deadline.

Thank you, Gerry Breshears, for graciously correcting my theology for nearly a decade and for always being willing to read and make notes on what I write. Thanks, also, to all the early readers of the manuscript as well: Jay Kim, Isaac Serrano, A.J. Swoboda, Joshua Ryan Butler, Daniel Kunkel, and Calum Hayes, who all provided essential feedback to make this the best book it could be.

Major thanks to Naseem Khalili, another early reader, who (as always) went the extra mile and got so excited about this book that I did too. It is a joy to work with you and know you and your family. Thank you for all your creative input and your consistent friendship to me, Ali, and Jude.

To Ryan Ingram, my pastor and boss at Awakening Church, for your unending support and leadership. Thank you for the unparalleled discernment you offer us, especially during this past year. We could not have navigated it without you.

Thank you to Jordan Chesbrough, my friend and co-conspirator in all things creative, for reading this and talking a ton about it, even before I showed you a word. I value every single thing you say.

Thank you to my mentor, Joel Dombrow, who I spared from reading this book, but continues to be my pastor twenty years later.

I also must acknowledge Kavin C. Rowe at Duke Divinity School for showing me the historical sources around Christianity and ideology. Without his lectures and seminars, this book would be missing a few important chapters.

This book is dedicated to my mom because she gave me a brain and life in the first place. Then, she stewarded it very well. Mom, I'm glad you forced me to read and always asked me tough questions and always supported environments of learning. You are the best mom ever and a gift to the lives of every person who gets the honor of knowing you.

And finally thank you, Awakening Church, for being such a thoughtful, beautiful community of Christians. We thank God, our Father, for all his gifts, and we saw a thousand of them as we worshiped with you.

About the Author

Chris Nye is a doctoral student at Duke University's Divinity School and the author of *Distant God* (Moody Publishers, 2016) and *Less of More* (Baker Books, 2019). For fifteen years, he has served as a local church pastor and is currently on a sabbatical. His writing has appeared in the *Washington Post, Christianity Today, The Gospel Coalition, Fathom Magazine,* and various other publications. He lives with his wife and son in Portland, Oregon.

You can connect with me on:
- http://chrisnye.co
- https://twitter.com/chrisnye

Subscribe to my newsletter:
- http://eepurl.com/gf77BT

Also by Chris Nye

Less of More: Pusuing Spiritual Abundance in a World of Never Enough

The US Constitution guarantees the right to the pursuit of happiness. But for most Americans, what this really means is the pursuit of more—more money, more prestige, more stuff. We've made idols out of innovation, growth, power, and wealth. Far from offering us happiness and satisfaction, this relentless pursuit of more has only left us exhausted, isolated, miserable, and wondering if there is a better way.

There is. *Less of More* exposes the American pursuit of more for what it truly is: an attempt to satisfy our souls with the temporary instead of the eternal. Pastor and writer Chris Nye invites us to consider what a full and abundant life looks like apart from money, status, and power. He exposes the lies inherent in our obsession with growth, fame, and wealth, and calls us to a countercultural life marked by connection, obscurity, vulnerability, and generosity.

For anyone who has gained the world but lost their soul, *Less of More* offers a compelling path toward a life of true, deep, lasting satisfaction with Jesus—not us—at the center of it.

Distant God: Why He Feels Far Away...And What We Can Do About It

There comes a time in every Christian's life when God feels distant. This feeling can be confusing, discouraging, or even dangerous.

Distant God meets us in the middle of this struggle. It helps us think rightly about what we're experiencing and gives practical ways for drawing near to God. It answers questions like:

What does it mean that God is always with me?

What role do works (like devotion, confession, and repentance) have in all this?

How should I handle spiritual lows and seasons of doubt?

When we feel distant from God, we need voices of truth speaking into our lives. Drawing from the story of the prodigal son, Chris Nye takes us through various reasons why we may feel this way and offers encouragement along the way.

This is not a book of trite answers or easy solutions, but it offers specific ways of drawing near when God feels distant. It also includes stories of Christians throughout history who have faced this issue in similar ways.

Distant God is a biblical and pastoral answer to why God might feel far away and what we can (and cannot) do about it.

Made in the USA
Monee, IL
22 July 2022